ECHOES OF TATTERED TONGUES

JOHN Z. GUZLOWSKI

Echoes of
Tattered Tongues

MEMORY UNFOLDED

AQUILA
POLONICA®
PUBLISHING

AQUILA POLONICA (U.S.) LTD.
10850 Wilshire Boulevard, Suite 300, Los Angeles, California 90024, U.S.A.
www.AquilaPolonica.com

ISBN (cloth): 978-1-60772-021-8
22 21 20 19 18 17 16   1 2 3 4 5 6 7 8 9 10

Printed in the U.S.A.
Library of Congress Control Number 2016930239

Acknowledgements:
Editor: Terry A. Tegnazian. Cover photo, cover design, interior book design and typesetting are by Ewa Wojciak, and are reproduced with permission. Photographs and other illustrative material are either in the public domain or reproduced with permission.

Photo captions and credits:

p. 8   – Author's parents, Jan Guzlowski (1920–1997) and Tekla Guzlowski (1922–2006), c. 1990s (credit: John Guzlowski)

p. 40   – Polish Triangle, Chicago, c. 1950s (credit: John Guzlowski, courtesy of Chuckman Chicago Nostalgia)

p. 100   – Royal Castle, Warsaw, October 1939 (credit: Archiwum Akt Nowych, Central Archives of Modern Records, Warsaw)

p. 154   – Author, his mother, sister and father, c. early 1960s (credit: John Guzlowski)

p. 158   – Author with his mother and sister, c. late 1950s (credit: John Guzlowski)

p. 165   – Author (credit: Linda Calendrillo)

Special thanks to Marek Zebrowski and Lidia Tułodziecka for their assistance with translations from Polish to English.

To
Linda, Lillian, and Luciana
The women in my life

CONTENTS

CONTENTS

CONTENTS

CONTENTS

"When the war started, we didn't know what war meant."
— Tekla Guzlowski

FOREWORD

In his preface to *Echoes of Tattered Tongues: Memory Unfolded*, John Guzlowski tells us that his immigrant survivor parents "couldn't spend a night without arguing with each other in Polish, the language of misery, poverty, and alienation." He explains that he ran from all this, ran for years, until his love for them—and his need to make sense of their anger at life and their frustration with each other—eventually pulled him back to their Polish language and the dark, brutal, impoverished world they had emerged from: the world that had almost killed them.

As a poet and witness, it was imperative that Guzlowski learn as much as possible about his parents' experiences during the war— what they saw, what they felt, and why those terrible things still held sway over them so many years later—concerns that have driven him, wounded him, and remained central to his work and to his life. And yet his search has not been for revenge for what his parents suffered in the slave labor camps, or even for what Poland suffered, but for the vein of gold in the broken, one-eyed man, his father, the gold in the unforgiving woman, his mother, and their rock-bottom goodness and courage.

Clearly, it was this need to know intimately what his parents lived through in the German camps, to be true to their experiences, that taught him how to write such unwaveringly lucid and luminous poems—poems that, line by line and syllable by syllable, leave his readers with no safe perches yet show them how to mourn and praise. Indeed, John Guzlowski has served as the chronicler of his parents' exploited bodies and the smashed bones of their martyred birth country. He set out to encounter that devastation and to understand it, and in this extraordinary book he has achieved that goal.

Charles Adès Fishman
Bellport & San Francisco, September 2015

PREFACE

Where I'm Coming From

I never set out to write about my parents and their experiences in the concentration camps in Germany and what it was like for us as immigrants here in America. When I was growing up, I wanted to get as far as possible away from them and that world.

When we landed at Ellis Island, we were unmistakably foreign. We didn't speak English. We dressed in black and brown wool that had been given to us by a UN relief agency. My mother wore a babushka on her head, my father a woolen cloth cap with a broken brim. They both wore their best shoes, leather boots that came to their knees. My mother's brother had stitched and hammered those boots by hand. All our belongings were gathered together in a small steamer trunk my dad had built.

We eventually settled in an immigrant neighborhood around Humboldt Park in Chicago. There I met Jewish hardware-store clerks with Auschwitz tattoos on their wrists, Polish cavalry officers who still mourned for their dead horses, and women who had walked from Siberia to Iran to escape the Russians.

It was a tough neighborhood, where I grew up, and our lives were hard: America then—like now—didn't much want to see a lot of immigrants coming over and taking American jobs, sharing apartments with two or three other immigrant families, getting into the kinds of trouble immigrants get into. We were regarded as Polacks—dirty, dumb, lazy, dishonest, immoral, licentious, drunken Polacks.

I felt hobbled by being a Polack and a DP, a Displaced Person. It was hard karma.

I started running away from my otherness as soon as I could, and for much of my life I continued to run. As I started moving into my early teens, I didn't want anything to do with my Polish parents and their past. I thought of it all as that "Polack" or immigrant past. It was so old world, so old-fashioned. I had parents who couldn't speak English, couldn't talk about baseball or movies, didn't know anything about Elvis Presley or Marilyn Monroe or James Dean, couldn't spend a night without arguing with each other in Polish, the language of misery, poverty, and alienation. I wanted to spend as little time as possible thinking about my parents and their Polishness and what my mother sometimes called "that camp shit."

I moved away from them, physically and psychologically and emotionally and culturally and intellectually. I stopped going to church, I left home, I didn't maintain my Polishness, I stopped speaking Polish, I stopped eating Polish food, I went to grad school, I immersed myself in American culture. I studied Emerson, Whitman, Thoreau, Dickinson, Eliot, John Dos Passos, Eugene O'Neill, Fitzgerald, and on and on.

I became the person my parents didn't want me to be. They wanted me to be a good Polish boy, going to church, living at home, dreaming of returning to Poland like my dad.

I guess I did what some immigrant kids always do. I said, your world is not my world.

And then it all changed: I started writing about my parents when I was in grad school. Maybe it was because I had finally gotten far enough away from them. Maybe not.

I realized very quickly that even if people don't want to read what I write, I had to write my poems about my parents just to make sure someone could. Really, there just aren't a lot of people writing about people like my parents and the other DPs. And if I don't write, who will? Imagine all of those hundreds of thousands of survivors who came to this country as DPs. They couldn't write for themselves.

At some level, I am writing for all the people who've sought refuge in America, whose stories were never told, whose voices got lost somewhere in the great cemetery of the 20th century—I feel that I have an obligation to listen to those voices and give them a place to be heard, to tell the stories they would write themselves if they could. For the last forty years, while I have been writing about my parents' lives, I am writing not only about their lives, but also about the lives of all those forgotten, voiceless refugees, DPs, and survivors that the last century produced, no matter where they came from.

All of history's "Polacks."

John Guzlowski
Lynchburg, Virginia, September 2015

My People

My people were all poor people,
the ones who survived to look
in my eyes and touch my fingers
and those who didn't, dying instead

of fever, hunger, or even a bullet
in the face, dying maybe thinking
of how their deaths were balanced
by my birth or one of the other

stories the poor tell themselves
to give themselves the strength
to crawl out of their own graves.

Not all of them had this strength
but enough did, so that I'm here
and you're here reading this poem
about them. What kept them going?

Maybe something in the souls
of people who start with nothing
and end with nothing, and in between
live from one handful of nothing
to the next handful of nothing.

They keep going—through the terror
in the snow and the misery
in the rain—till some guy pierces
their stomachs with a bayonet

or some sickness grips them, and still
they keep going, even when there
aren't any rungs on the ladder,
even when there aren't any ladders.

Half a Century Later

BOOK I

Dreams of Unhurried Memories

Too many fears
for a summer day
I regulate my thoughts
and my breathing
regard the humidity
and dream

Somewhere my parents
are still survivors
living unhurried lives
of unhurried memories:
the unclean sweep of a bayonet
through a young girl's breast,
a body drooping over a rail fence,
the charred lips of the captain of lancers
whispering and steaming
"Where are the horses
where are the horses?"

Death in Poland
like death nowhere else—
cool, gray, breathless

The Wooden Trunk

When my parents, my sister and I finally left the refugee camp in Germany after the war, we were allowed to bring very little, only what would fit into a steamer trunk. The problem was that we couldn't afford to buy one. Not many of the families living in the camps could. You can imagine why that was, so my father did what other people did. He and a friend got together and built a trunk.

Someplace, somehow, they found a hammer and a saw, nails and some metal stripping, and they set to work. Getting the wood wasn't a problem. They got the wood from the walls of the barracks they were living in. It was one of the old German concentration-camp barracks that had been converted to living space for the refugees, the Displaced Persons, and this place didn't have finished walls of plaster, or anything like that. If you wanted a board, you could just pull it off the wall, and that's what my father did.

I don't think he felt guilty about busting up those walls. He had been a prisoner in Buchenwald Concentration Camp for four years, and he'd spent enough time staring at them, so he probably felt he could do anything he wanted to them, and it would be okay. I think if a man spends enough time staring at a thing, finally it becomes his by a kind of default. I don't know if that's what my dad thought. He didn't say a lot about building that wooden trunk, and he probably didn't give it much thought.

The trunk my father and his friend built out of those old boards wasn't big. It was maybe four feet wide, three feet tall, and three feet deep. The walls of the trunk were about three-quarters of an inch thick. But wood is always heavy, so that even though it wasn't real big, that trunk generally needed two people to lift it. My father, of course, could lift it by himself. He was a small man, a little more than five feet tall, but he had survived four years in Buchenwald as a slave laborer. That taught him to do just about any work a man could ask him to do.

My parents couldn't get much into the trunk, but they put into it what they thought they would need in America and what they didn't want to leave in Germany: some letters from Poland, four pillows made of goose feathers, a cross made of wood, a black skillet, some photographs of their time in the DP camps, some clothing, of course, and wool sweaters that my mother had knitted for us in case it was cold in America. Somewhere, I've got a picture of me wearing one of those sweaters. It looks pretty good. My mother knitted it before her eyes went bad, and she was able to put little reindeer and stars all over that sweater.

When we finally got to America, my parents didn't trash that wooden trunk or break it up, even though there were times when breaking it up and using the wood for a fire would have been a good idea, kept us warm. Instead, they kept it handy for every move they made during the next forty years. They carried it with them when we had to go to the migrant farmers' camp in upstate New York where we worked off the cost of our passage to America. And my parents carried it to Chicago when they heard from their friend Węglarz that Chicago was a good place for DPs, for refugees. And they carried that trunk to all the rooming houses and apartment buildings and houses that we lived in in Chicago, in the area that was then known as the Polish Triangle. I remember in those early days in Chicago there were times when the only things we owned were the things my mother and father brought with us in that trunk, and the only furniture we had was that trunk. Sometimes it was a table, and sometimes it was a bench, and sometimes it was even a bed for my sister and me.

When we were kids growing up, my sister Danusia and I played with the trunk. It had large blocky letters printed on it, the names of the DP camp we came from in Germany, the port we sailed from, and the port we sailed to in America. We would trace the letters with our fingers even before we could read what they said. We imagined that trunk was the boat that brought us to America, and we imagined that it was an airplane and a house. We even imagined that it was a swimming pool, although this got harder to imagine as we got older and bigger.

When my parents retired in 1990 and moved from Chicago to Sun City, Arizona, they carried that trunk with them. That surprised me because they didn't take much with them when they went to Arizona. They sold or gave away almost everything that they owned, almost everything that they had accumulated in thirty-eight years of living in America. They got rid of bedroom suites and dining room suites, refrigerators and washing machines, ladders and lawn mowers. My parents were never sentimental, and they didn't put much stock in stuff. They figured it would be easier to buy new tables and couches when they got to Sun City.

But they kept that trunk and the things they could put in it.

And a TV set.

After my father died in 1997, my mother stayed on in Arizona. She still had the trunk when she died. She kept it in a small, 8 foot x 8 foot utility room off the carport. My parents had tried to pretty the trunk up at some point during their time in Arizona. The original trunk was bare unpainted wood, and was covered with those big, blocky, white letters I mentioned. But for some reason, my parents had painted the wooden trunk, painted it a sort of shiny dark brown, almost a maroon color; and they had papered the bare wood on the inside of the trunk with wallpaper, a light beige color with little blue flowers.

When my mom died, I was with her. Her dying was long and hard. When she finally died, I had to make sense of her things. I contacted a real estate agent, and he told me how I could get in touch with a company that would sell off all of my mother's things in an estate sale.

I thought about taking the wooden trunk back with me to my home in Valdosta, Georgia. I thought about all it had meant to my parents and to me, how long it had been with them. How they had carried it with them from the DP camps in Germany to Sun City, Arizona, this desert place so different from anything they had ever known overseas.

I knew my sister Danusia didn't want the trunk. I called her up, and we talked about the things my mother left behind and the estate sale and the trunk. Danusia has spent a lifetime trying to forget the time in the DP camps and what the years in the slave labor camps during the war had cost my parents.

But did I want it?

I contacted UPS about shipping it, what it would cost, how I would have to prepare the trunk. They told me it would cost about $150 to ship.

But did I want it?

I finally decided to leave it there in Sun City and to let it get sold off at the estate sale. That wooden trunk had been painted over, and the person buying it wouldn't know anything about what it was and how it got there. It would just be an anonymous, rough-made trunk, painted a dark brown, almost maroon color, with some goofy wallpaper inside.

Thinking back on all of this now, I'm not sure I know why I left that trunk there. When I'm doing a poetry reading and tell people the story of the trunk and read one of my poems about it, people ask me why I left it. It doesn't make any kind of sense to them. And I'm not sure now that it makes any kind of sense to me either.

So why did I leave it?

I was pretty much used up by my mom's dying. It had been so hard. My mother went into the hospital for a gall bladder operation and had had a stroke, and the stroke left her paralyzed, confused, and weak. She couldn't talk or move, and the doctor told me that my mother couldn't even understand what was being said to her.

Her condition got worse pretty fast, and I put her in a hospice in Sun City. I sat with her there for three weeks, watched her breathing get more and more still. Sometimes, her eyes would open, and she would look around. I would talk to her then about things I remembered, her life and my father's life, my life and my sister's life. I don't know if she understood anything. She couldn't blink or nod, or make sounds with her mouth. I just talked to her about what I remembered, any stupid thing, the bus rides we took, the TV shows she always watched, the oleanders she and my dad liked to plant and grow in the backyard. I didn't think that there was much else I could do for her.

When she died, I didn't want to do anything except get back home to my wife Linda in Georgia. Maybe the extra burden of figuring out how to carry that trunk back to Georgia was more than I could deal with. Or maybe I thought that trunk wasn't the same trunk that my parents had brought from the displaced persons camp in Germany. It had been painted, changed.

Or maybe I just wanted that trunk to slip away into memory the way my mother had slipped away, become a part of my past, always there but not there.

My Parents Retire to Arizona

They give us things we don't want: blades
for hacksaws I don't own, canna lily bulbs
in Ziploc bags even though I am death on them,
four cans of Comet cleanser, gold bottles
of dishwasher detergent, paintings of places
they've never seen (in one, three laughing friends
in blue snowsuits stand on skis on a mountain
while a fourth skis away laughing), a mason jar
filled with pennies, Kennedy half-dollars,
and an old quarter my dad insists is silver.

"Please," my mom says, as she searches
the basement for more, "please, take these things."

We shrug and take everything they offer.

We know what they cannot say:
"Think of us as you use these things.
Once we were as young as you, cleaning
the house, dreaming over a backyard
of bright red lilies, counting these pennies."

A Good Life

My father says
in time he'll learn
to listen to the Polonaise
and not hear Sikorski
or Warsaw, the hollow surge
and dust of German tanks,

only Chopin,
his staff of clean notes
and precise legato.

His dreams will be
of crystalled trees,
papered gifts
in red half light,
the smell of warm sheds
and girls drawing milk
from waiting cows.

The snow will fall
and go unnoticed.

Windows Without Scars

When I tell my mother
in the desert kitchen
the war was fought
to teach me something

her fingers carve space
into a room without seams
and she nods like a priest
who can't recall

the bread made with ashes
the penance she asks for
the days in her belly
waiting to be born

My questions dry out
become the dust
blowing through her voice
and I see three beggars

in gray wool dancing
circling the coffin
singing charity
will save you from death.

What My Father Believed

He didn't know about the Rock of Ages
or bringing in the sheaves or Jacob's ladder
or gathering at the beautiful river
that flows beneath the throne of God.
He'd never heard of the Baltimore Catechism
either, and didn't know the purpose of life
was to love and honor and serve God.

He'd been to the village church as a boy
in Poland, and knew he was Catholic
because his mother and father were buried
in a cemetery under wooden crosses.
His sister Catherine was buried there too.

The day their mother died Catherine took
to the kitchen corner where the stove sat,
and cried. She wouldn't eat or drink, just cried
until she died there, died of a broken heart.
She was three or four years old, he was five.

What he knew about the nature of God
and religion came from the sermons
the priests told at mass, and this got mixed up
with his own life. He knew living was hard,
and that even children are meant to suffer.
Sometimes, when he was drinking he'd ask,
"Didn't God send His own son here to suffer?"

My father believed we are here to lift logs
that can't be lifted, to hammer steel nails
so bent they crack when we hit them.
In the slave labor camps in Germany,
He'd seen men try the impossible and fail.

He believed life is hard, and we should
help each other. If you see someone
on a cross, his weight pulling him down
and breaking his muscles, you should try
to lift him, even if only for a minute,
even though you know lifting won't save him.

My Mother's Hair

Her hair is not brown, not white.
It is the color of grief, the color
Of bones washed clean by death.

She combs it and it gives her
No pleasure.

Once her mother combed it.

She remembers this,
And the way she braided it.

She loved the touch
Of her mother's hands on her neck,
The smell of her so near.

She remembers the way
The soldiers kicked her mother
After shooting her in the face.

The blood on the floor
The blood in her hair.

My Father's Mother Asks Him to Forget the War

My father sits at the table listening
to the photos spread before him.
The last one whispers, I am your mother,
hold me, I am dying, remember
that spring when your father died
before the war, before my death
became mixed with your dying.

I dressed in black, sold flowers
in the village, felt myself dying
in tongues and prayed for deliverance
for your birth, for you to hold me,
to remember me, nothing else mattered.

I knew it then and know it
still, just hold me, look at my face
make sense of the life I lived,
just hold me, hold me, anything.

My Mother Talks About the War

I. My Mother Reads My Poem
"Cattle Train to Magdeburg"

She looks at me and says,
"That's not how it was.
I couldn't see anything
except when they stopped
the boxcars and opened the doors

And I didn't see
any of those rivers,
and if I did, I didn't know
their names. No one said,
'Look, look this river
is the Warta, and there
that's the Vistula.'

What I remember
is the bodies being
pushed out—sometimes
women would kick them out
with their feet.

Now it sounds terrible.

You think we were bad women
but we weren't. We were girls
taken from homes, alone.
Some had seen terrible things
done to their families.

Even though you're a grown man
and a teacher, we saw things
I don't want to tell you about."

II. How Her Mother and Sister Died

Sometimes, my mother says, her home
West of Lwów comes back to her in dreams
That open in grayness with the sounds
Of a young, flowered girl in white
Singing a prayer of First Communion,
The dirt streets around the church pure
With priests and girls and boys.

The singing prayer leads her to the grave
Where her mother and her sister Genia
And her sister's baby daughter lie,
The marshy grave where the hungry men
Dropped them after shooting them
And cutting them in secret places.

My mother says, these men from the west
Were like buffaloes: terrible and big.

She waves the dreams away with her hand
And starts again, talking of plowing the fields
Of cutting winter wood, of that time
When the double-bladed axe slipped
And sank a wound so deep in her foot
That she felt her heart would not
Jar loose from its frozen pause.

III. The Beets

My mother tells me of the beets she dug up
In Germany. They were endless, redder
Than roses gone bad in an early frost,
Redder than a grown man's kidney or heart.

The first beet she remembers,
She was alone in the field, alone
Without her father or mother near,
No sister even. They were all dead,
Left behind in Lwów. The ground was wet
And cold, but not soft, never soft.

She ate the raw beet, even though
She knew they would beat her.

She says, sometimes she pretended
She was deaf, stupid, crippled,
Or diseased with typhus or cholera,
Even with what the children called
The French disease, anything to avoid

The slap, the whip across her back
The leather fist in her face above her eye.
If she could've given them her breasts
To suck, her womb to penetrate
She would have, just so they would not
Hurt her the way they hurt her sister
And her mother and the baby.

She wonders what was her reward
For living in such a world? It was not love
Or money. She can't even remember
What happened to the Deutsche Marks
The American sergeant left that day
In the spring when the war ended.

She wonders if God will remember
Her labors. She wonders if there is a God.

IV. Liberation

My mother has the peasants' view of the world:
Disorder and chaos, roads that end
In marshy fields, chickens that begin
To bleed from the mouth for no reason.
Nobody makes movies of such lives,
She says, and begins to tell me the story
Of when the Americans first came,
Of the sergeant who stood with a suitcase
In the yard between the barracks.

He was shouting, screaming.
They didn't know what he wanted
And feared him. One of the women
Came out (first, she hid her children
Under the bed) and then another.
They knew he wasn't a German.
When fifteen of them stood in the yard,
He opened the suitcase, emptied
Its Deutsche Marks on the ground,
Said in broken German, "This is for you,
Take it, this is the money they owe you."

And then the British soldiers came,
And put them in another camp,
Where the corpses still had not been buried,
Where the water was bad, where my mother
Got sick, where her stool was as red
As the beets she had to dig every day.

And my father worked hard, sawing
The wood, getting ready for winter,
Like he did in Poland. He knew this work
And did it for her and the children,
My sister and me. But the British
Moved them again, to another camp,
And they had to leave the wood, even though
My father tried to carry some on his back.

And it was cold in the new place, and many
Of the babies died, and my sister was very sick,
Maybe from drinking the dirty water.

V. What the War Taught Her

My mother learned that sex is bad,
Men are worthless, it is always cold
And there is never enough to eat.

She learned that if you are stupid
With your hands you will not survive
The winter even if you survive the fall.

She learned that only the young survive
The camps. The old are left in piles
Like worthless paper, and babies
Are scarce like chickens and bread.

She learned that the world is a broken place
Where no birds sing, and even angels
Cannot bear the sorrows God gives them.

She learned that you don't pray
Your enemies will not torment you.
You only pray that they will not kill you.

Why My Mother Stayed with My Father

She knew he was worthless the first time
she saw him in the camps: his blind eye,
his small size, the way his clothes carried
the smell of the dead men who wore them before.

In America she learned he couldn't fix a leak
or drive a nail straight. He knew nothing
about the world, the way the planets moved,
the tides. The moon was just a hole in the sky,

electricity a mystery as great as death.
The first time lightning shorted the fuses,
he fell to his knees and prayed to Blessed Mary
to bring back the miracle of light and lamps.

He was a drunk too. Some Fridays he drank
his check away as soon as he left work.
When she'd see him stagger, she'd knock him down
and kick him till he wept. He wouldn't crawl away.

He was too embarrassed. Sober, he'd beg
in the bars on Division for food or rent
till even the drunks and bartenders
took pity on this dumb Polack.

My father was like that, but he stayed
with her through her madness in the camps
when she searched among the dead for her sister,
and he stayed when the madness came back in America.

Maybe this was why my mother stayed.
She knew only a man worthless as mud,
worthless as a broken dog, would suffer
with her through all of her sorrow.

A Garden in the Desert

At the end
my father sat in his garden
in the early morning

the desert in Sun City,
Arizona, that strange place,
still cool

the clear light
tinged with desert blue

the pigeons cooing.

He couldn't lift
the shovel then, drag
the bag of topsoil
from here to there.

He couldn't breathe
or stand either.
There wasn't much
left to him.

But he could nod
toward an orange tree,
its roots bound in burlap,
and point to the place
where he wanted me
to plant it.

There, he'd say
to me in Polish,
please plant it there.

My Mother's Optimism

When she was seventy-eight years old
and the angel of death called to her
and told her the vaginal bleeding
that had been starting and stopping
like a crazy menopausal period
was ovarian cancer, she said to him,
"Listen Doctor, I don't have to tell you
your job. If it's cancer it's cancer.
If you got to cut it out, you got to."

After surgery, in the convalescent home
among the old men crying for their mothers,
and the silent roommates waiting for death
she called me over to see her wound,
stapled and stitched, fourteen raw inches
from below her breasts to below her navel.
And when I said, "Mom, I don't want to see it,"
she said, "Johnny, don't be such a baby."

Six months later, at the end of her chemo,
my mother knows why the old men cry.
A few wiry strands of hair on her head,
her hands so weak she can't hold a cup,
her legs swollen and blotched with blue lesions,
she says, "I'll get better. After his chemo,
Pauline's second husband had ten more years.
He was playing golf and breaking down doors
when he died of a heart attack at ninety."

Then my mom's eyes lock on mine, and she says,
"You know, optimism is a crazy man's mother."

And she laughs.

At the End: My Father

I. My Father Dying

His death like all death
is hard. There is no peace
in the darkness. His right eye,

the one that sees, is looking
for someone to comfort him.
He knows his mother is dead

but he whispers for her still,
the way he did as a boy
crying at her deathbed.

In his Polish the word
is three long, pleading
syllables: "*Mamusia.*"

The second syllable
is stressed, the third
falls off into silence.

Just yesterday, he talked
a little, asked for water,
smiled, when I gave him some.

But today, he can only
call for his mother. Hope is
the cancer no drug can cure.

II. Pigeons

My father dreams of pigeons,
their souls, their thin cradles
of bone, but it is their luck

he admires most. A boy in Poznań
in a dawn all orange and pinks,
his hands opened like a saint's

and taught those birds to fly, to rise
on the air, their wings beating
the rooftops into flesh, into dreams

of angels above the crystal trees.
And later in the gray dawn clouds
blowing about him in the camps,

where not even pigeons were safe,
where his body, thin then,
like a shoelace, sought other dreams

other bodies, and found only
the comfort of worms—even then
he could still remember

the birds without chains,
breathing quickly and cooing
"We are going, we are going."

III. A Sonnet about Dying

My mother sat next to my father
in the hospital, all the time holding
his hand, whispering "Janek, Janek,"
the name his mother called him,
but still he wept and struggled to loosen
the straps around his hands and feet.

In the corridor, there was some noise,
and my mother looked up.
Four nurses stood there talking.
One of them smiled and then laughed,
and the others started laughing too.

My mother looked at me, nodded slowly,
and said, "Half of us are going to the grave,
and the other half to a wedding."

At the End: My Mother

I. My Mother Prays for Death

She is the poet of dead-ends, old despairs
written in whispers, beads slipping between
her fingers like peas dropping into soup.
In her hands, the rosary is a ring of bones,
yellow as old ivory, hard as living.
Her wooden suitcase holds nothing.
She doesn't need what she leaves behind:
the empty house, the worthless bed,
the pictures she gathered over the years.

These photos are memories, and memories
belong to someone else: the daughter
who will not speak to her, the husband
who died believing in a God she can't
imagine, me the foolish son who dreams
somewhere of violins, of snow falling
like soft sand on a prairie, of children
waiting for the sound of a key in a lock.

If her husband and her daughter and I
were there now beside her in her room,
she'd ask, "Why are we born, why do we die?"
She'd say, "If you could answer these questions,
I'd answer all the others." They are easy.
They come from a land of simple faces, of blue
novelty drinks topped with paper umbrellas,
of dinners that are almost never illusions.

Where she comes from, a mother's screams
last longer than a photograph, longer
than bronze shoes, and everything's lost
the way a penny's lost in the dirt at our feet.
Sorrow is the only gift God bestows.

II. How Can I Ask My Mother?

Her left hand clutches the sheet,
pulling it tight across her chest,
and her breathing is liquid, full of phlegm,
a gurgling that reaches deep inside me
like a spoon stirring and stirring.

This is all that's left of her: this breathing
and this hand, the one stirring
and the other holding tight,
clutching the sheet like a boat
on the ocean that is her dying.

I can't ask her if she wants to die.

III. Dying in a Blue Room in Arizona

I wait for my mother to stand
and sing about the young girl
who stares into the deep well
and dreams of her lover
whose blood gives life
to the poppies on Cassino

and to call me *Johnny* again
and take my hand and dance
an arm-twirling polka the way
she did when I was six
and she could not have yet
dreamed her own dying
nor all the distances between us

I want her to tell me
Mój Boże, co będzie, będzie,

And I want to believe
That these words are some kind
Of grace that will free her
From this ocean of tears.

[Translation: *Mój Boże, co będzie, będzie* means My God, What will be, will be.]

Souls Migrating in the Rain

Patiently,
They wait for the rain—
Not for its wetness
But its dark grayness

It covers their flight.
Otherwise,
I would go out
And try to stop them,
Bring them back
To where I think
They belong,

Here in this house,
Sitting, old before the TV,
Watching Wheel of Fortune,
Vanna's blue gown
A whirl of skies—

Or sitting there
On the patio
Like fishermen,
Their coffee growing cold
Beside them

But no,
They leave in the rain,
So I can't see them leaving

Someday,
I will understand
That this is right
Understand this
After they leave me

Like the sea
On a moonless night
Growing away from me,

Its waves moving first toward me
And then away, toward me
And then away

Refugees

BOOK II

Refugees

We came with heavy suitcases
made from wooden boards by brothers
we left behind, came from Buchenwald
and Katowice and before that
Lwów, our mother's true home,

came with our tongues
in tatters, our teeth in our pockets,
hugging only ourselves, our bodies
stiff like frightened ostriches.

We were the children in ragged wool
who shuffled in line to eat or pray
or beg anyone for charity.

Remembering the air and the trees,
the sky above the Polish fields,
we dreamt only of the lives waiting
for us in Chicago and St. Louis
and Superior, Wisconsin

like pennies
in our mouths.

The Happy Times and Places

My father was a man plagued by nightmares about the German concentration camps he and my mother both spent years in. When I was a child, his screams would wake us all. I don't think I've ever heard screams like that. They were muffled in an odd way. Screams, in my experience, are usually accompanied by an explosion of air. My father's nightmare screams were drawn in. Even in his sleep, it was almost like he was afraid to scream. I would come to my father's bedroom, and he would be asleep and screaming and struggling in his sleep with the German guards who were beating him. He drank all the time to keep these nightmares back.

My mother's experiences in the camps showed themselves in a different way. She was afraid of so many things, loud noises, whistling, even clowns she saw on TV; and she was especially afraid of things being done incorrectly. She would beat and scold all of us, even my father, if the table was set the wrong way for dinner or if we came home late after an outing. My sister and I often thought that our parents were crazy; our lives amid the screaming and fear and anger just didn't make sense to us.

But despite all of this, I now realize that my parents wanted so hard to give us happiness. And when I think about my childhood, I think about the happy times my parents tried to give us, and I think about the special places where these happy times took place.

For me, the most important of these moments took place on the June day I turned four years old, a Sunday in 1952, when I ran to the garden at the back of a little house we were renting in Chicago and stood there among black-eyed Susans with their yellow petals and long, thin necks. And my mother in a white dress with little blue flowers sat in the garden between me and my sister, and my father stood in front of us with a Brownie box camera.

He was asking us to smile in the Polish we still spoke at home, while my mother told me about the day ahead, how we would go to Kiddie Land, an elaborate children's playground, and my sister Danusia and I would ride on the blue and yellow and red cars and the roller coaster built just for kids. My mother made it sound like there was something special about being a kid, the way she talked about the day we had planned.

It makes a picture I don't want to forget.

I think we all have such special perfect times and such happy places, where we feel most ourselves, most comfortable. Maybe we remember these special places and special times and turn to them because they were the places and times our parents were happy, before their lives took their inevitable turns. Maybe not. Like most of us, I'm not good at figuring out the complex why of things.

But I remember that particular Sunday morning when I was four; you remember sitting at a baseball game between your mother and father, and both are yelling at one of the players in a way that frightens you just a little but you know is okay; or you remember a day when your parents took you swimming and your mother was laughing at your father because he was wearing her bathing cap pulled down over his eyes in a silly way; or you remember your father sitting at the piano with a cigarette between his lips, playing some slow, sad piece you loved so much while, in another room, watching and listening, your mother stood washing some dinner plates or ironing some clothes.

First Snow

I still remember the first time
I saw snow. I was almost three,
living in a refugee camp in Germany.

One night after dinner, I looked
out the window and saw snow
falling thick and fast on a convoy
of army trucks moving through the camp.

I'd seen them before, the trucks
taking mothers and fathers
and children like me to other camps,
other countries, but not the snow.

I stepped outside into the night
without my jacket or shoes on.
I didn't know the snow would be
cold and wet, but that didn't matter.

I stood in the white swirling snow
and stretched out both my hands
to catch the falling wonder.

My Mother Tells Me How She Met My Father

I first saw him in front of the barracks. He was walking with six other prisoners, a German soldier behind them pushing at them with some kind of rifle. Your father wasn't how he is now. He was skinny then, like two shoelaces tied together.

I was not such a prize after three years in the camps either. When the Americans came, they weighed me and found I was less than a hundred pounds—and what was I wearing? You want to know? Woolens on my legs, a gray rag to hide my hair, a striped dress.

And him? Your father? Like I said, skinny with a bleeding towel across his face from where he lost his eye.

Still, he walked up to me, took my hand, and said in Polish, "*Proszę pani.*"

Yes, he said, "Please, miss," and like a proper gentleman, he clicked his heels. I thought he was at least a count, maybe a prince.

Then just before your dad had a chance to kiss my hand, the German behind him kicked him in the pants and said, "*Dummkopf, raus!*" *Get moving, dummy!*

Your father was like that. Always putting on airs, even then in the camps talking of Polish honor as if he and Poland shared a soul.

Really, he was worthless. I wish he had left me there in the camp. He couldn't drive a car, he couldn't fix a leaky roof.

When I asked him in the refugee camp to help me pack to come to America, he took a little drink and bundled all the clothes together in a bedspread like America was across the street.

The fool, I should have kicked him like the German soldier did when I met him.

Instead, I kissed him and wept.

The Day I Was Born in the Refugee Camp

My mother washed her face in cold water, tied her hair back, and put on an old dress. She said she knew my birth would be hard, that she had given birth before, to my sister, and that then the dirt had flushed out of her body like a rabid dog that had finally snapped its chain. She said as well there had been storms the day before I was born, and the creeks near the refugee camp were running high, and some of the barracks near the river were evacuated.

She said she was alone that day I was born. My father had seen my sister Danusia being born two years earlier, and he wept and said to my mother that he couldn't go through that again. So she told him he should just leave, take the money they had and go buy himself some vodka or whiskey, find a barn he could crawl into and drown himself in the drink, drown himself until he couldn't hear her screams or see the mess that was coming.

There was no hospital, no doctor, no nurse, no midwife, no one with her to help her with the darkness and the screaming when I started to come. There was just me and the tearing in her stomach and her bones breaking apart like God had decided to squeeze her until she was nothing but blood exploding through her useless skin in His dirty hand.

And feeling it, feeling the river of shit and squeezing and bones breaking, she remembered the road that brought her there to that refugee camp in Germany and that darkness.

She remembered the Germans who killed her mother and raped her sister and kicked her sister's baby to death, and the years in the slave labor camp when the guards would promise her a potato if she would suck them, a piece of meat if she would fuck them, and she remembered being thankful for the food.

She remembered too the time after the war when the other women in the refugee camp struggled to hold onto their babies because they knew that giving birth to them would kill them because their wombs were still in the war, still weak and tortured and beaten, still kicked and stabbed and wounded, still bleeding and crying and hoping, still falling and slipping and starving, still kneeling and begging and weeping, still everything that had happened since the day the Germans put her and the girls from her village on the train to bring them to this Germany where every birth was a struggle in the mud for a breath.

And she screamed then and knew that screaming was useless, and so she screamed again and kept screaming until the flood came and my bones poured from her flesh like tomatoes exploding in the hands of a dirty God who didn't care about what she remembered or feared or wept over.

She knew that all He wanted was to hold another life in His hand, and that nothing she could beg for would change the way He turned the baby, regarded it, and let it live or not.

Lessons

There is no sky
only Ellis Island
the docked ship
rusting rising
falling as we wait
for my father

lost somewhere
in the crowd of DPs
in cast-off babushkas
black-market khaki
the gray wool
that froze
before Moscow
and cracked

he left to buy
sausage and bread

has America
already taught him
his first lesson:
there is no sausage
in America

and what is the second:

that a Polack
who traded an eye
for survival can
die in a compound
so close to New York
that even his son,
knowing nothing
of Cohan, Jolson,
Keeler, can hear
their syncopated
whispers, the silver
of their tapping
cakewalks.

My Father's First Day in America

It was as if the world poured
Into his one good eye. He saw
Sidewalks, steel buildings, a single
Airplane in the sky, a little girl eating

A piece of bread with jam, another
Drinking something red out of a bottle,
A priest consulting his watch before
Crossing a street, a sheet of newspaper

Blowing sideways, two drunks dancing
A heavy-footed leaping dance,
So many cars not even an educated man
Who could count could count so many,

Men in suits with suitcases so small
A child could carry four or five of them
Even to Moscow or Magdeburg,
Women in dresses so light the slightest

Wind would reveal every bone
And the curving flesh around it,
Their beauty so pure he felt his hands
Open and his palms turn to them.

And he asked the blessed world before him
in a Polish it would never understand,
"Why did they do it, drag us off,
kill us, and keep us chained for so long?"

Promised Land

I. Coming to America, 1951

When I ask my mother now
what we had when we came
from the camps in Germany,
she shrugs and starts the list:

some plates, a wooden comb,
some barley bread, a crucifix,
four goose-down pillows
and a frying pan, a letter from
a friend in America.

We were poor as mud,
she says, and prayed for little:
to find her sister, to work,
to not think about the dead,
to live without anger or fear.

II. The Farms of Buffalo, New York

In the orchards that first fall,
my parents picked apples,
red ones sweet as white sugar,
and my sister and I waited near
the ladders to catch the apples
before they touched the ground,
but our hands were small, the apples
big and hard. They came so fast,
like stones thrown by bad boys.

We begged our mother to please
let us go back home to the refugee
camps in Germany. We'd be good.
We'd be careful when we picked
the strawberries in the spring.
We wouldn't stop till we were done,
and we promised we'd never cry
if she'd let us go back.

But her heart was stripped to bone,
and she told us if we didn't work,
we would die in Buffalo.

III. Winter in America

She remembered the German cold,
winters that broke the souls
of old people and left children
frozen like wheat stalks
in the fields, hollow reeds
the winds and ice blew through.

In Buffalo, there was cold too.

Picking the apples in late October,
she felt it on her hands and feet,
remembered the wooden shoes
she wore in the slave camps, how cold
the frozen wood was on her skin
as she dug for beets in Germany.

She knew nothing about America
but thought that maybe farther west,
there wouldn't be so much snow.

Looking for Work in America

I. What My Father Brought With Him

He knew death the way a blind man
knows his mother's voice. He had walked
through villages in Poland and Germany

where only the old were left to search
for oats in the fields or beg the soldiers
for a cup of milk. He knew the dead,

the way they smelled and their dark full faces,
the clack of their teeth when they were desperate
to tell you of their lives. Once he watched

a woman in the moments before she died
take a stick and try to write her name
in the mud where she lay. He'd buried

children too, and he knew he could do
any kind of work a man could ask him to do.
He knew there was only work or death.

He could dig up beets and drag fallen trees
without bread or hope. The war taught him how.
He came to the States with this and his tools,

hands that had worked bricks and frozen mud
and knew the language the shit bosses spoke.
.

II. I Dream of My Father as He Was When He First Came Here Looking for Work

I wake up at the Greyhound Station
in Chicago, and my father stands there,
strong and brave, the young man of my poems,
a man who can eat bark and take a blow
to the head and ask if you have more.

In each hand he holds a wooden suitcase
and I ask him if they are heavy.

He smiles, "Well, yes, naturally. They're made
of wood," but he doesn't put them down.
Then he tells me he has come from the war
but remembers little, only one story:

Somewhere in a gray garden he once watched
a German sergeant chop a chicken up
for soup and place the pieces in a pot,
everything, even the head and meatless feet.
Then he ate all the soup and wrapped the bones
in cloth for later. My father tells me,
"Remember this: this is what war is.

One man has a chicken, and another doesn't.
One man is hungry, and another isn't.
One man is alive, and another is dead."

I say, there must be more, and he says,
"No, that's all there is. Everything else
is the fancy clothes they put on the corpse."

III. His First Job in America

That first winter
working construction
west of Chicago
he loved the houses,
how fragile they looked,
the walls made of thin layers
of brick, the floors
just a single planking
of plywood.

A fussy, sleepy child
could destroy such a home.
It wasn't meant to witness
bombing or the work of snipers
or German 88s.

He worked there
until the cold and wind
cut him, and he found himself
thinking for hours of the way
he stacked bricks in the ruins
of Magdeburg and Berlin.

Finally, he quit
not because he was afraid
but because he knew
he could without fear

his shovel left
standing at an angle
in a pile of sand.

Polish Triangle, Chicago

We lived in a single room, slept
on the floor, went to the bathroom
outside like in the refugee camps,
but no one here spoke German.

At night we stared out the window
at the cars in the street. They struggled
in the snow where a green bus
sank into a white hill tall as a cow.

My father hugged me and said,
"In the spring the snow will melt
and turn to water," and I asked him
will the water be like the sea,
will a bus take us back to Buffalo
or will we sail on the hard gray waves
all the way back to Germany.

My mom said, "This is America,
and here's where we'll stay."

All the Clichés About Poverty are True

Our first refugee winter in Chicago
my dad came home with a box of wood scraps
he traded some guy in a bar for a drink
and maybe a couple packs of cigarettes.

Me and my sister Danusia made houses
with those clean-smelling blocks and wedges,
pushed them around the floor like they were horses,
trains, and cowboys. My father that night

put them into the wood stove in the kitchen
for a little warmth, but it wasn't enough.
My mom raised her hand and said she'd spank us
if we didn't stop crying for the blocks.

I don't remember what we did the next night.
Maybe we burned our crayons and chairs.

Friends in America: A Sonnet about Charity

The women who came to our apartment
didn't speak Polish, and the only English
my parents knew was "Thank you, Missus,"
but they came and brought dresses for my mother,
rubber boots for my father, cans of pork
and beans and loaves of bread for all of us,
and for my sister and me, comic books
and sometimes a hard rubber toy, a doll
or a red truck with a missing tire.

We didn't know who they were or how
they'd found us or even their real names.
But they had names: "*dobra*" and "*fajna*,"
and we knew what those words meant.
These were "good" and "fine" women.

A Letter to My Mother from Poland, October 4, 1952

Dearest Tekla, my only sister,

The war has been over for so long but still we suffer the leavings of war. We have tables but no food, pain but no medicine, strong metal beds but no straw to sleep on.

Each day I wait for night to free me from the longing but it only brings me dreams of our dead mother crying about the wash, blaming me for the dresses I can't get clean. I hold them above the tub but haven't the strength to lower them into the water.

Sometimes, I see her standing in the doorway looking east toward the autumn forest where snow already falls. Perhaps if you could come back to Poland and travel back to the village with me, maybe we could find the grave where they dropped her and Genia and Genia's baby. Someone there must know where they are buried. Maybe then mother would stop coming to me.

If you could come in the spring, perhaps you could bring me a bolt of blue cloth, blue with little white flowers. You know the kind we wore the year before the war. A new dress for summer would be so nice.

Your loving sister,
Zofia

My Mother's Sister After the War

I.

She was young once
and knew life was short
and that what she did
in the refugee camps
with the consumptive boy
didn't matter.

They made love in the dark
among the rushes, his body—
thin as a worm—saying,
I'm here, take my past,
dream of me when I'm dead.

She could hear nothing,
see nothing, think only
that the grave he walked into
did not speak to her.

She turned from it
the way a woman will turn
from her lover when she
has found peace, the center
of silence in the movement
of flesh and the slow
swelling release of blood
from the walls of the vagina.

II.

Later, she came back
to the farm, to the cows
moving slowly on the flat
gray plain as they searched
for grass in the Polish rain,
came back to the preparations
she would have to make
for herself and the baby.

Her fear grew heavier,
like a fat uncle who feeds
on all she has to offer
until finally all belongs
to him and she is left,
a fear-starved child
whose bones pray for a visit
of flesh while fearing
that he will ask
for the bones as well.

At night in the kitchen
her fingers lay empty
on the table. The boy
was gone. She felt
the heat of his fingers
along her ribs—the smell
of his breath on her neck,
of his death on her breasts.

This was not madness.
She had been mad before
in the camps, felt objects change
their position, their shape,

the stove from there
move here, the floor
become a thing of dreams.

III.

Often in church, she sat
in silence, without shame,
her face turned from the altar.

She knew there were things
that happened that
were no one's fault.

She was the feast of marzipan,
soup made from duck's blood,
a lamb roasted slowly
and with great care
for King Sobieski
or Marshal Piłsudski
or the Baby Jesus.

They had no answer
for the pain. It gripped
her chest the way a cruel man
grips and shakes the child he loves.

IV.

She wondered,
What if there is only darkness?

Memories scored in black ink
and scattered paper—her mother
folding into herself weeping
with a letter in her hand?

Her father receiving the blows
that first would scar him
and later kill him?

Her sister watching
the baby kicked to death?

What then?
What then?

V.

She thinks the final circle
around her grave will be small,
her aunt from Lwów,
her brother, and her sister
if they are still alive.

The pain—it is so strong
she cannot feel the doctor's
scissors nor hear his words.

She thinks he speaks
the language of mules.

Later in the Promised Land

My mother took her deaths hard
and quiet. She hid her mourning
in the bedroom, the door closed.
Behind it her grief turned to anger,
and her anger turned to fear.

She feared everything, the sky
in the morning, a drink of water,
a sparrow singing in a dream.

She feared my father's love
and faith, and she beat him.
She feared my sister's love
and need, and she beat her.

She feared my love, and taught me
love was the thing you left behind
in the mud on the side of a road.

Me in America, 1952

I pretend I'm a baby
walk on all fours, see things
I don't understand, a couch,
a lamp, a new refrigerator.

Later, my hassock seat
is a blue boat in a white ocean
the waves higher than
the trees in the front yard

and I think about the lost girl
in the story my father told me:
why was she in the wrong forest,
was the girl dark like the children
who live next door in the red house,
why did the witch spin in her rags,
dance a polka and then fall down?

Later, I look out the window
and see a penny in the grass.
When I go outside to get the penny
it is not there, but when I stand
again at the window, there it is.

I wonder who I will be
in the story my father will tell
when he comes home from the factory
where he makes white string
like the string in my shirt.

Will I be the sister
who runs away, or King Sobieski
riding a blind horse
searching for her
in the yellow mountains?

Later, I bake bread in the TV set
and kiss everything in the house,
the dirt in the flower pot
tastes like chocolate,
the carpet hurts my lips.

Later, I am a rabbit
and a father afraid of robbers
and I grow wings and fly
to the ceiling above my head.

Stories My Sister Danusia Told Me

I. Poor Adaś

Adaś is sad.
His father is dead.
His mother works hard
but she makes very little.

Adaś always
comes to school
in worn-out clothes
and he is always hungry.

He doesn't have money
to buy books or pencils

But the good children
don't forget about Adaś.

They share
their bread with him
and sometimes

they buy him a pencil.

God loves these children
and He loves their parents too.

II. Sweet Little Birds

Hungry birds
sit on the window sill
and look in.

The good children
stop playing with their dolls
and red balls and rubber trucks

and they open the window
and give the birds some bread.

They will never forget

III. The Storm

The storm clouds
hide the heavens
and the thunder is loud,
and black and green clouds
roll toward the children.

The sparrows hide in trees
or under the eaves of roofs.

The children run from the garden
where they have been watering
the beautiful red flowers.

They fear the flash of lightning
and the way it strikes the trees
but their grandmother tells them
not to cry because "God watches
over good children and sparrows,
and soon the storm will end
and the sun will shine again."

Friends in America: Polack Joe's Story

My dead father was an evil man. He'd
drink till he was crazy, vodka spitting
from his nose, my mother pleading
with him to stop, praying to Baby
Jesus to help her bring him home.

Once in a bar on Division Street
he took a fountain pen and stabbed
her in the face so hard the silver
point pierced her cheek and blood
filled her mouth and reddened her teeth.

The bartender there was this big guy,
virile, a real bull. Tough as Jesus.
This guy lost a hand in the streets of Warsaw
when he slammed a homemade bomb
into the tread of a German tank. When he saw
my mother's cheek, heard her long
liquid scream, he put his rubber hand
to his eyes and fainted like a school girl!

My old man was like that, solid crazy.
He'd wake me up at night, cut me
with a strap, and chase me naked
through the alleys. My wife begs me,
Pray for him, Joey, make his soul free
so he can fly to Heaven. But I won't pray.
I don't want no part of a Heaven or a God
that'll take a guy like that.

When I tell my wife this, she cries.
She asks me don't I ever want to see
my dead father again. I say no. I won't pray.

I say they could sell our baby girl
to the whores in the park so they could
cut open her belly and eat what's inside
before I pray. I say God can nail our son
to an iron crucifix before I say one
prayer to save my father from the fire.

I understand what my wife wants.
I know. I used to get on my knees
with the other Polacks at St. Fidelis

The pews there were like a ladder
that led to the incensed altar.
We prayed our guts out. For what?
For ashes, palms, and three more
"Our Fathers" and a dozen "Hail Marys."

But let me stop talking already
about my father and all his foulness.
Let me dance for you instead.

I'll be good as a girl from Poland,
a pure country girl from a village
somewhere west of Częstochowa,
a girl who dreams Jesus can still
save her from this world, lead her
through corridors that lead to sunsets
like ladders lead to heaven above.

Look here my friends, my brothers.
Like the wounds of Jesus on my face
you can still see the scars
where my father struck his claws!

The Stories My Grandmother Told My Mother

In their log house in the forests
west of Lwów, my grandmother
told my mother tales in the winter
to pry her thoughts from the sound
of trees splitting with the cold,
exploding with a crack like that
of her father's double-barreled shotgun

A cat, she would say, can't be trusted.
It comes in the short spring night
and sleeps on the priest's chest
watching his Adam's apple
as if it were some mouse hidden
under a blanket of stubbled skin
and then striking its sudden claws
through his skin into cartilage

And what of the wolves, she'd ask,
the nine wolves that in the winter's
gray stone dawn would smash
their bones against the door,
hammering like hungry seals
until the door splinters and the baby
is got at—even from the cradle
even from its precious sleep?

And listen, Tekla, my mother's mother
would whisper then, there are men
as bad as wolves that no door
—no matter how solid the oak—
will keep out.

So trust in Jesus
in the world of clouds far beyond
the frozen forests of this frozen world

Do this always, and fear the greedy hens.

Family Life After the War

When I was a kid,
I sat among
The broken bones
And sorted them
into piles.

My parents watched
And nodded.

Put that one there,
They would say.
The other
By the wall.

Sometimes
My father's weeping
Made it hard to know
If he wanted to keep
A bone or throw
It away.

That's when I'd
Ask my mother
And she'd just
Wave her hand
And tell me
I was a fool.

Fussy Eaters

Fifty years later, my mother says,
Johnny, remember how you wouldn't eat
the good Polish sausage your father brought
from Staszek's Deli? Such a fussy eater

and your sister Danusia was worse. In the camps,
she would chew on a stick from morning
to night and beg on her knees to get
some of the breast milk I was saving for you

because the doctor said you were a goner.
Not till I came to America did I understand
what he meant by this word. A goner—yes.
But in America, Danusia wouldn't eat

the sweet cabbage with vinegar and onions
or the dumplings cooked with hot butter.
Only ten, she'd look me hard in the eyes—
like I was a stone dropped from the sky—

and say, I can't eat this Polack food.
It's gray and tough and laced with veins that steal
my breath away so much I feel like choking.
And I would say to her, But you'd eat

Marzipan, and one time I slapped her
and gave her five dollars—this in a time
when you'd work hard all day for five dollars—
and she went to Rickey's Restaurant

and ate meatloaf and mashed potatoes
and came home and was sick in the toilet.
This made me happy, and I said to her,
Now, you'll eat my cooking. Now, you'll like it.

Whistling

My mother always said whistling
in the house whistles the devil in.

Even if you whistle low, you'll hear
his knuckles nicking on the door,

hollow like the sound a pig's snout
makes knocking against the bucket

that holds its slop. You'll hear
his nicking even if you whistle

like a happy child sitting
near a stove reading comics.

Nothing will keep the devil out,
she says. Even if you pray to Jesus

you'll hear Satan's wooden knock
or feel him smiling in the cloud

of dark stars inside your head
when you try to sleep in your bed.

A Young Soldier from Częstochowa

In his dreams
my father cradles
the boy in his arms

his skin is white
already

his arms gone
at the shoulders

his blood
on the dreamer's
hands and face

My father wipes it
from the boy's eyes
And holds him
closer

Here's What My Mother Won't Talk About

Just a girl of nineteen
with the grace of flowers
in her hair

coming home
from the pastures
beyond the woods
where the cows drift
slowly, through a twilight
of dust, warm and still
as August

She finds her mother
a bullet in her throat
her sister's severed breasts
in the dust by her feet
the dead baby
still in its blanket

It all ends there
not in the camps
but there

Ask her

She'll wave her hand
tell you you're a fool
tell you

if they give you bread
eat it

if they beat you
run

Chores

One day I asked my mother,
"How about an allowance.
for sweeping these stairs?
A quarter once a week?"

My mother gave me a hard look
and told me in the old country
kids slaughtered pigs on their own
with wooden hammers and drained

the black lumpy blood
from the carcasses and made
Polish sausage from the guts
every day of the week

for nothing, not even a quick
thanks a lot in Polish.
And then she said to me,
"If you won't do the chores

unless I pay you, then don't."
And she grabbed my broom,
and went outside and stopped
the first kid she saw on the street,

a kid I hated from school,
and she gave him a quarter
just for doing the stairs
I would've done for free.

Friends in America: The Polish Captain of Lancers

His wife loved the captain for his wounds,
The red shrapnel scars across his chest,
The fingers broken by the Germans,
The way he held his head cocked and still
As he listened to Chopin or talked of those
Who died around him among the rocks
Below Monte Cassino in the spring
When the Poles finally moved toward
The abbey's fallen bricks and ruined walls.

She listened with her fingers across her lips
When he told her who the fallen men were,
The orphan from Poznań who never learned
Anything but killing. The mandolin player,
Older than the others, who played the songs
The boy from Beaumont, Texas taught him,
The corporal who left Poland before the war
And came back because everything was lost,
And the others, men who needed to take
The hill the way hungry men dreamed
Of bread and needed to feel it in their hands.

She listened to the stories a hundred times,
Every time he'd come home from the bars
On Division Street where soldiers would still
Sing the song the survivors sang about the battle.
The song's words were simple, of red poppies
Growing among the fallen walls and bricks
Getting their blood from the blood of those
Who fell where crosses would later stand.

She loved the captain for the way he always
Cried for Poland, but she didn't love the drinking,
The cognac he'd take straight from the bottle
When he thought nothing could make him sadder
And he needed it more than some need bread.

And finally when she found him drunk
And crying and singing about the poppies
Growing red with the blood of Polish boys
She forced the bottle into his mouth, saying
"If you want to drink so much, drink" and held
That position until he choked to death.

Danusia

Do you remember those Sundays
Driving with mother and father
In that big gray DeSoto to the bars
On the prairie north of Chicago?

You asked me, your little brother,
To dance to Hank Williams singing,
"Hey, good looking, Whatcha got cooking?"
And we twirled and jitterbugged,
Waltzed and stepped beneath the blue
and green Christmas tree lights.

Did the drunks turn from their dreams
Of Normandy with its gray sands
And the Ardennes with its frozen dead
To watch us dance the way they danced
When they were children before the war?
Did they know that we were DPs,
The children they fought in Remagen
To free? Did they turn and clap,
Toss us nickels and Mercury head dimes?
And what did we talk about as we danced?

I'm sure it wasn't about the way
Mother slapped you across your face,
Chased you screaming through the rooms,
Or swung for you under the bed
With the broken broomstick handle.

Listen, I am thinking of you still
And praying that you forgive me
For never telling you that I knew
How bad she hurt you
And if there was some way
I could dance with you again
Beneath those blue and green lights
I would, and I would beg you
In my broken Polish not to cry.

Proszę Danusia,
Proszę nie płacz.

[Translation: *Proszę Danusia, Proszę nie płacz* means Please Danusia, Please don't cry.]

Friends in America: Murdertown

I.

My friends were beaten,
stabbed, pulled from their bikes
and cars and knocked into the street.

One of my friends was dragged
out of his house by a gang
and beaten unconscious with clubs.

He was a good boy, kind of
sissy-like with long hair
and a soft voice but a good boy.

He was in the hospital
for about a month.
He didn't want to ever leave it.

The papers called the area
Murdertown.

II.

One time, a man was shot dead
in front of my house.

When I went outside
to see what the police were doing,
a cop called me a motherfucker
and told me he'd throw
my ass in jail
if I didn't get back home.

I was 12.

I went back into the house
and never stepped outside again
when someone was shot
in front of my house.

III.

I carried a switchblade in my pocket.
Twice I used it on somebody
so that they wouldn't hurt me.

Once it was a friend,
who was just joking around.
He jumped out of an alleyway
when he saw me passing.
I didn't know he was joking,
and I stabbed him in the stomach.

When I couldn't get a knife,
I carried a hammer or a baseball bat.
The hammer was better, lighter,
and I could put it in my belt.

IV.

Every couple years there were riots.
Mostly in the summer.
One time it was so bad
that Mayor Daley, the old one,
felt the cops needed some back-up
so he called in the National Guard.

The soldiers drove around
the neighborhood in jeeps
with loaded machine guns.

Nights, you'd hear the shooting,
see flames rolling off stores
and apartment buildings
burning just south of us
on Division Street.

V.

Three of the priests in my old parish
were convicted years later
of being pedophiles.

They heard my confessions
and told me to say three Hail Marys
and three Our Fathers.

They weren't interested in me.
I wasn't pretty enough for them.

VI.

One time a gang attacked my mom and me
when we were coming home from the store.
This was in the early afternoon.
It was bright and warm.

We were carrying shopping bags,
and they wanted to steal our food.

My mother beat one of the gang boys
down to the sidewalk.
He tried to crawl away,
but she kept kicking him
and kicking him.

He pleaded with his homeboys
to come save him from my mom.
They wouldn't come.
They were afraid.

Finally, my mom stopped kicking the gang boy,
and she let him crawl away.

My mother had survived three years
of life in a concentration camp,
and she knew how to get by
in the streets of Chicago,
in our old neighborhood.

VII.

We finally had to move
when the house we'd been living in
was burned to the ground
during a gang war in the early '70s.

Nobody ever rebuilt on that spot.

It's still an empty lot
in Murdertown 42 years later.

The Evil that Men Do

My mother is not God
not the Blessed Virgin
not some saint you pray to
when all else in life fails you
and you're hanging onto hope
the way you hang onto the hand
of a loved one who is dying.

My mother has a clay heart,
a golem heart. She'll say
you're stupid if you buy
smoked fish not fresh.
She'll beat you with a broom
if you disobey or are awake
when she comes from working
nights in the factory's molding room.

At nineteen she came home
to the bodies of her mother,
her sister, and her baby
murdered by the Germans.
At twenty, things happened
she still won't talk about.

My mother talks about
the usual camp shit: eating
beets and wormy potatoes,
wearing frozen wooden shoes
that left both feet crippled,
the cold nights, and the face
of the moon above the wire.

Maybe she learned it there
in the slave labor camps—
how to cut herself loose
from you with a slap
or an ugly word like *kurwa*
or *dupa Jasiu* or *gnoju*.

I've seen her take my father—
stupid from work and drink—
and pull him from the chair
and kick him while he cried:
"*Tesia, Tesia, mój Boże.*"

She forgives the Germans
for teaching her this discipline
but she can't forgive my dad,
my sister Danusia or me.

We breathe too easy.

[Translation: The Polish curse *kurwa* means whore; *dupa Jasiu* means foolish
asshole; and *gnoju* means filthy shit.
The phrase "*Tesia, Tesia, mój Boże*" translates as "Tesia, Tesia, my God." "Tesia" is
diminutive for Tekla, my mother's name.]

My Father's Prayer

Dear Baby Jesus,
If You have any pity left
bestow it, please, on my wife.
She suffers from the war.

You know about her mother,
and her sister and the baby,
and about the things
she's told no one.

Me? I have my whiskey,
and the fighting.

When my sorrow is great
I go to the taverns
on Division Street
and drink and fight
with the Americans,
men who are bigger
and harder than me.

I thank them
for beating me
till I can't remember
the sorrow.

But my wife Tekla
she is one of your sparrows
and the pain she feels
has nowhere to go.

So she beats our daughter
sweet Danusia
and is cruel to our son
who she also loves.

My wife's a good woman
but like all of us
she has seen
terrible things.

Two Worlds of Language

I. Missing Pieces

They look at you and make assumptions:
you're from Chicago, you know the rules
to baseball, you have grandparents who live

in Kansas, you get the music of the Twenties,
you know what to wear when you go to church,
your dad doesn't eat pickled pigs' feet

with vinegar. And then you do something
that throws them off. Maybe you don't get a joke
or the subtext of a familiar phrase.

This always happens to me, especially in class
when I'm teaching. A student says something,
and I just don't get it and everyone else does,

and then there I am, once more staring
through my silence at a world that speaks
a language I'll never master.

That's when they know that you're odd, different.
I laugh it off, tell them I'm a non-native
speaker, and they're puzzled for a moment

and don't know if I'm joking or what.
But outside class, a person will feel my difference
is just a little too much, and he'll turn away.

II. Dumb Polacks

Good children, we played outside
while our tired mother slept inside
resting from working the night shift,
and then a boy came along.

A bully, he was big and hard
and threw the ball at us
again and again, and called us DPs
and Dumb Polacks. Frightened

we called to our mother softly
in the English we didn't know
and had only practiced in whispers,
"Mother, Mother, Mother."

She had no English at all
and didn't come, and the boy
kicked us till we both were screaming,
"Mother, Mother, Mother."

Back in the house later,
with our tears and fearfulness,
we told her what happened
and she said, "Why didn't you call?"

We just stood there in silence.
What could we say to her?

III. Kitchen Polish

I can't tell you about Kant
in Polish, or the Reformation,
or deconstruction

or why the Germans moved east
before attacking west,
or where I came from,

but I can count to ten, say hello
and goodbye, ask for coffee,
bread or soup.

I can tell you people die.

It's a fact of life,
and there's nothing

you or I can do about it.
I can say, "Please, God,"
and "Don't be afraid."

If I look out at the rain
I can tell you it's falling.
If there's snow,

I can say, "It's cold outside
today, and it'll most likely
be cold tomorrow."

IV. My Grandparents

There are no photographs
of who they were
what they did

One was beautiful
with hair like the sun
setting in late August
but more pale

Another was slow, a third fat
with fingers so strong
they never let go

The last, a wanderer
who became lost searching
for work in Galicia

They come to me
as I sit after breakfast
in the kitchen
and I tell them
the truths I have found

Time is a windmill
the world exhales each day
inhales each night

Friends come to us
when we are dying
or struggling with mysteries
or joyfully shedding our skin
in summer on a beach
somewhere

Don't worry, I tell them,
we are never alone

And I tell them stories,
true ones, like this:

Once in an airport
while I sat alone, writing
a poem about Primo Levi's
death in Turin

An Asian woman walked
back and forth near me
singing deep in her throat

de   de   tay
        de de   tay   tay
            de   de   tay

and she stayed by me
singing

singing

until I finished
the lines about Levi's
guilt and forgiveness
in the moment before
he threw himself down
to his death
on the stairs
in Turin

She did not see me
hearing her song
as she walked there
singing

her song
as deep in her throat
as Jesus or love
as deep in my throat
as it was in hers.

de   de   tay
      de de   tay   tay
            de   de   tay

And when I tell my grandparents
this story, they sit
in their brown suits
and dark babushkas, smiling

and nodding as if they
understood my words, as if
my English was their Polish.

The Old Country

They'll never see home again, these old Poles
with their dreams of Poland. My father
told me when I was a boy that those who tried
in '45 were turned back at the borders

by shoeless Russians dressed in rags and riding
shaggy ponies. The Poles fled through the woods,
the unlucky ones left behind, dead
or what's worse wounded, the lucky ones

gone back to wait in the old barracks
in the concentration and labor camps
in Fallingbostel or Wildflecken
for some miracle that would return them

to Poznań or Katowice. But God
wasn't listening or His hands were busy
somewhere else. Later, in America
these Poles gathered with their brothers

and with their precious sons and daughters
every May 3, Polish Constitution Day,
to pray for the flag. There was no question
then what the colors stood for, red for all

that bleeding sorrow, white for innocence.
And always the old songs telling the world
Poland would never fall so long as poppies
flower red, and flesh can conquer rock or steel.

Refugees never learn what their children always
learn. Those left behind in the old country
leave the past behind. Borders stay open
only in the dreams of those dying on this side.

The War

BOOK III

Landscape with Dead Horses, 1939

I.

War comes down like a hammer, heavy and hard
flattening the earth and killing the soft things:
horses and children, flowers and hope, love
and the smell of the farmers' earth, the coolness
of the creek, the look of trees as they unfurl
their leaves in late March and early April.

You smell the horses before you see them.

II.

Horses groan, their heads nailed to the ground
their bodies rocking crazily, groaning
like men trying to lift their heads for one
last breath, to breathe, to force cold air
into their shredded, burning lungs.
For these horses and the men who rode them,
this world will never again be the world
God made; and still they dare to raise their heads,
to force the air into their shredded lungs.

III.

Look at this horse. Its head torn from its body
by a shell. So much blood will teach you more
about the world than all the books in it.
This horse's head will remake the world for you—
teach even God a lesson about the stones
that wait to rise in our hearts, cold and hard.

September 1, 1939: The Day World War II Began

When you read about history in the history books, it's all so clear. The numbers make it seem that way. Numbers, people say, don't lie. A thing begins on a certain date, and it ends on another particular date. You see the beginning of a thing, and you see its end. It all seems neat and clean, but it isn't really.

The history books, for instance, tell us that World War II began on September 1, 1939 when the Germans invaded Poland from the west, and the same books tell us that the war in Europe ended almost six years later on V-E day, May 8, 1945.

My father Jan Guzlowski was not a student of history. He never had any kind of formal education, never went to school, never could read much beyond what he could read out of a prayer book, but he knew history. He had lived through history. He was only 19, working on his uncle's farm in Poland, when the Germans invaded and turned his whole world upside down. I guess you can say he learned history from the ground up. He was captured by the Germans in a roundup in 1940 and sent to Germany. Like a couple of million other Poles, he spent the next five years at hard labor in concentration and slave labor camps there.

But for him, the war didn't end when his camp was liberated sometime at the end of March 1945, and it didn't end on Victory-in-Europe Day, May 8, 1945, and it certainly didn't end when my family finally came to America as refugees, Displaced Persons, in June 1951.

The war was always with him and with my mother Tekla Guzlowski, a woman who spent three years in the slave labor camps in Germany and before that had seen the other women in her family raped and murdered by the Germans. The trauma of what she had seen never left her. When I was growing up, I could see it in her eyes and the way she held herself together.

My parents carried with them the pain of war and its nightmares every day of their lives.

In 1997, fifty-two years after the war ended, when my father was dying in a hospice, there were times when he was sure that the doctors and the nurses trying to comfort him were the German guards who beat him when he was a prisoner in the concentration camp. There were also times when he couldn't recognize me and my mother and sister. He looked at us and was frightened. He thought we were there to torture him.

In 2005, toward the end of my mother's life, I told her that I was going to be giving a poetry reading and that I would be reading poems about her and my father and their experiences in the war. I asked if there was something she wanted me to say to the audience.

"Yes," she said, "Tell them we weren't the only ones."

My parents knew that the war had always been with them, teaching them the hard lessons, teaching them how to suffer grief and pain, how to be patient, how to live without hope or bread, how to survive what would kill a person in the normal course of life.

The war taught them that war has no beginning and no end.

Fear (A Poem Based on a Story by Tadeusz Borowski)

During the war, there was only work and death.
The work broke you down, filled your stomach
with rocks and threw you in the river to drown.
The work shoved a bayonet up your ass
and twisted the blade till you were dead.

In the camps, there was only what we ate
and those we worked with—sometimes women.
But we never made love. I'll tell you why.

Fear. I remember once a thousand men
were working a field with sticks, and trucks came
and dumped naked women in front of us.
Guards were whipping them to the ovens,
and the women screamed and cried to us, pleaded
with their arms stretched out—naked mothers,
daughters, and sisters, but not one man moved.

Not one. Fear will blind you, and tie you up
like nothing else. It'll whisper, "Just stand still,
soon it will be over. Don't worry, there's nothing
you can do." You will take this fear to the grave
with you. I can promise. And after the war,
it was the same. I saw things that were as bad
as what happened in the camps. I wish
I had had a gun there. I would have
pressed it here to my forehead, right here.
Better that than what I feel now. This fear.

My Mother Before the War

She loved picking mushrooms in the spring
and even when she was little she could tell
the ones that were safe from the ones that weren't.

She loved climbing the tall white birch trees
in the summer when her chores in the garden
and the kitchen were done. She loved to ride
her pet pig Caroline in the woods too
or sit with her and watch the leaves fall
in the autumn. She felt that Caroline
was smarter than her brothers Władzio and Jan,
but not as smart as Genia, her sister
who was married and had a beautiful baby girl.

My mother also loved to sing.
There was a song about a chimney sweep
that she would sing over and over;
and when her father heard it, he sometimes
laughed and said, "Tekla, you're going to grow up
to marry a chimney sweep, and your cheeks
will always be dusty from his dusty kisses."
But she didn't care if he teased her so.

She loved that song and another one,
about a deep well. She loved to sing
about the young girl who stood by the well
waiting for her lover, a young soldier,
to come back from the wars far away.

She had never had a boy friend, and her mom
said she was too young to think of boys,
but Tekla didn't care. She loved the song
and imagined she was the girl waiting
for the soldier to come back from the war.

My Father Before the War

He thought he would always live
according to the seasons and holy days
that came regularly like the ringing
of bells from the church steeple
in the village north of Poznań.

He'd put on the blue suit his uncle
gave him when he turned 16
and wash his hands and walk to church.

A good boy, he always loved going there
on Holy Saturday to have the food,
the eggs and butter, the salt and bread,
blessed with Holy Water by the priest.

My father loved going early to church
on Easter Sunday, leaving the farm
with his aunt and uncle before the sun
was a pink silence over the east,

and coming to the church where little girls
in their white dresses stood holding lilies
while the boys seemed serious and awkward
in the suits handed down by their older brothers.

And my father loved May Day when he pledged
his hands and heart and soul to Mary,
the mother of Jesus, and he loved Pentecost

when he imagined the tongues burning
like candle flames in a darkened church
above the heads of the apostles, and he loved

Christmas with its mysterious midnight mass
that began in darkness and ended in light,
and the Feast of the Three Kings and more.

He imagined this would always be the life
he lived in his holy village north of Poznań.

There Were No Miracles

Men died where they stood

Children were left
for the dogs and the pigs

Schoolgirls came home
to find their mothers dead
their fathers with necks cut

Priests sat at their tables
wondering if they should
kill themselves

Some of them did

Others hid in the forests
till hunger and fear
brought them back
to the villages
and the trains
that would take them
to death

and some took their crosses
with them

but others left them
in the stations
where they'd prayed
for miracles.

The German Soldiers

I. German Soldiers Moving East

Birds wheel in the sky, a soft
Maelstrom of feathers and wings,
Screeches and caws. You'd think
They were angry lovers the way
They circle on their black hot wings
Above the burning synagogue,
The wolf smoke rising from it
And sending a message even
The trees and the wind can read:
We are here and we are coming.

It is all beautiful now and will be
More beautiful as the sun sets
And night draws purple veils
Across the western horizon,
The door to the home we love.

In the darkness, softly, you'll hear
The quick sound of a mandolin
Playing something, perhaps a tango
From the beer halls of Magdeburg.

On your skin you'll feel the wind
Of the future in the rising beat
Of every note we soldiers sing,
Our dancing bodies a storm of arms,
Legs, and helmets before the sparks
That rise like stars into the dark night.

Soon, with the gray light of morning,
We will march away, further east,
And the ashes will grow cold
With no one around to feel
The heat and weight of our leaving.

II. German Soldiers Come to a Polish Village

On their knees, and one by one, each man
and woman, each child, is shot and falls
backward without a sound into the mud
like an iron rod. God doesn't love these people.

They live in darkness, thatch their low cottages
with straw, burn wet wood in mud stoves
like evil children in a fairy tale.

There is no fat for their lamps. The sole light
you see comes from a candle in a cellar
where a woman in rags searches for roots.

This is the only world they'll ever know:

these huts, and the mud road that brought us here
and will take us out again when we are done.
This is where we gather them, here on this road.

Listening to their screams and pleading
we know these people will never again
drink from their pond or make shoes of straw
or eat a filling meal of sausage and bread
or laugh like children laugh alone in the dark.

We soldiers are only human. We love
to kill. It is the hidden God in each of us.

III. German Soldiers Stealing from the Dead

We take their shoes,
their shirts, their pants,
their wallets and hats.

We take their belts
and the food they cook.

We take their teeth
capped with gold,
their guns and ammo.

We leave behind
their eyes and fingers
their ears and breath
their legs and feet
their hearts and dreams.
They're worthless.

IV. What the German Soldiers Left Behind

Dead fathers and dead mothers,
Children so frightened they wet themselves,
Priests in black wool standing

In fields also black,
Old men holding babies
Not their own,

Trains, stores, sparrows,
Rows of tombstones, haystacks,
Benches, synagogues, trees,

Carousels, real horses
Lying dead on the street of stones,
Ballooning bigger and bigger,

A bus also dead in the street,
A woman in a moment of shame
Asking the way to a church,

An umbrella, a street vendor's cart,
Some horseradishes (who was selling them,
Where has he gone, was he a Jew, a Pole,

A German from Silesia?)
A door with a broken lock,
One wool cap and then some others,

A quiet man, too shy to look
At the man who paid him
For the paper and smiled,

A large metal pot with dented sides,
A young girl, perhaps twelve,
Who a minute before had been reading

A narrow street, three canes,
Seventy-eight books in a wooden stand,
Most bound in leather, some in paper.

All gone now, gone in flames
And everything else is waiting
For the end of everything else.

My Mother Was 19

Soldiers from nowhere
came to my mother's farm
killed her sister's baby
with their heels
shot my grandma too

One time in the neck
then for kicks in the face
lots of times

They saw my mother
they didn't care
she was a virgin
dressed in a blue dress
with tiny white flowers

Raped her
so she couldn't stand up
couldn't lie down
couldn't talk

They broke her teeth
when they shoved
the dress in her mouth

If they had a camera
they would've taken her picture
and sent it to her

That's the kind they were

Let me tell you:
God doesn't give
you any favors

He doesn't say
now you've seen
this bad thing
but tomorrow
you'll see this good thing
and when you see it
you'll be smiling

That's bullshit

Cattle Train to Magdeburg

My mother still remembers

The long train to Magdeburg
the box cars
bleached gray
by Baltic winters

The rivers and the cities
she had never seen before
and would never see again:
the sacred Vistula
the smoke-haunted ruins of Warsaw
the Warta, where horseflesh
met steel and fell

The leather fists
of pale boys
boys her own age
perhaps seventeen
perhaps nineteen
but different
convinced of their godhood
by the cross they wore
different from the one
she knew in Lwów

The long twilight journey
to Magdeburg—
four days that became six years
six years that became sixty

And always a train of box cars
bleached to Baltic gray.

My Father Talks about the Boxcars

The train would slow, and then stop
And we would wait for the doors
To grind open so we could see
Where we were, and sometimes

There would be children in the fields
Bent over boards or a broken plow
And we would beg them for water
And they would say, "Dear Jesus,

If we only could, but the Germans
Would shoot us," and we would beg
The children to tell us where we were
And we'd ask if they knew where

The tracks led—and they'd whisper,
the tracks went west to Germany
And maybe further but they didn't know,
Maybe to America or France.

And we would watch with hungry eyes
the doors grind back and close.

Grief

My mother cried for a week, first in the boxcars
then in the camps. Her friends said, "Tekla,
don't cry, the Germans will shoot you
and leave you in the field," but she couldn't stop.

Even when she had no more tears, she cried,
cried the way a dog will gulp for air
when it's choking on a stick or some bone
it's dug up in a garden and swallowed.

The woman in charge gave her a cold look
and knocked her down with her fist like a man,
and then told her if she didn't stop crying
she would call the guard to stop her crying.

But my mother couldn't stop. The howling
was something loose in her nothing could stop.

A Cross of Polish Wood

Told to take nothing
my father took the cross
his mother had given him
two clean-planed strips
made one by four nails
and a figure in lead

But he didn't pray in the box cars.
He whispered and listened
to whispers—
talk of Polish honor
and the strength of lances
of Anders and Sikorski—
and someone always said
"Poland will never fall
Panzers are only made of steel"

The fall of Poland taught him to pray
sent him to his knees in Buchenwald
to the nails and the lead
and the clean-planed Polish wood.

My Mother's First Winter in Germany

My mother never thought she'd survive that first winter. She had no
coat, no hat, no gloves, just what she was wearing when the Germans
came to her house and killed my grandma and took my mom to the
camps.

A soldier saved her life there. He saw her struggling to dig beets
in the frozen earth with her hands, and he asked her if she could
milk a cow.

She said, "Yes," and he took her to the barn where the cows were kept
and raped her.

Later, the cows kept her from freezing and gave her milk to drink.

Sisters in the Labor Camps

They ate
what the Germans
gave them

soup that was always
too thin, meat alive
and gray

with maggots,
bread made from sawdust
and sorrow,

and they looked
at each other
with the same cold eyes

and feared that nothing,
not even love,
would keep them
alive till spring.

Hunger in the Labor Camps

I. What My Father Ate

He ate what he couldn't eat,
what his mother taught him not to:
brown grass, small chips of wood, the dirt
beneath his gray dark fingernails.

He ate the leaves off trees. He ate bark.
He ate the flies that tormented
the mules working in the fields.
He ate what would kill a man

in the normal course of his life:
leather buttons, cloth caps, anything
small enough to get into his mouth.
He ate roots. He ate newspaper.

In his slow clumsy hunger
he did what the birds did, picked
for oats or corn or any kind of seed
left in the dry dung by the cows.

And when there was nothing to eat
he'd search the ground for pebbles
and they would loosen his saliva
and he would swallow that.

And the other men did the same.

II. What a Starving Man Has

He has his skin. He has a thinness
to his eyes no bread will ever redeem.
He has no belly and his long muscles
stand out in relief as if they'd been flayed.

He is a bony mule with the hard eyes
one encounters in nightmares or in hell,
and he dreams of cabbage and potatoes
the way a boy dreams of women's breasts.

They come uncalled for, round and fevered
like rain that will never stop. There is always
the empty sea in his belly, rising
falling and seeking land, and next to him

there's always another starving man who says,
"Help me, Brother. I am dying here."

III. Among Sleeping Strangers

The moon set early and it grew darker,
and the men settled to sleep in the cold
without blankets. Soon it would be spring
but it was still cold, and it was always cold

at night, and they did what men always did
at night when they were cold. They pressed their bodies
together and looked for warmth the way a man
who has nothing will look, expecting nothing

and thankful to God for the little he finds,
and the night was long as it always was
and some men crawled roughly across the others
to reach an outside wall to relieve themselves,

and some men started coughing and the coughing
entered the dreams of some of the other men
and they remembered the agony
of their mothers and grandfathers dying

of hunger or cholera, their lungs coughed up
in blood-streaked phlegm, and some men dreamt
down deeper and deeper against the cold
till they came somehow to that holy moment

in the past when they were warm and full
and loved, and the sun in those dreams rose early
and set late and the days were full of church bells
and the early spring flowers that stirred their lives

and in the morning the men shook away
from the cold bodies of their brothers
and remembered everything they had lost,
their wives and sisters, their lovers, their homes

their frozen fingers, their fathers, the soil
they'd been born on, the souls they'd been born with,
and then they crawled up out of the earth
and gathered together to work in the dawn.

IV. The Germans Who Owned Them

These men belonged to the Germans
the way a mule belonged to the Germans
and the Germans stood watching

their hunger and then their deaths,
watched them as if they were dead trees
in the wind, and waited for them to fall,

and some of the men did. They sank
to their knees like children begging
forgiveness for sins they couldn't recall,

or they failed to rise when the others did
and were left in the wet gray fields
where the Germans watched them

and the Germans stood watching
when the men who were still hungry
came back and lifted the dead men

and carried their thin bones to the barn,
and buried them there before eating the soup
that wouldn't have kept them alive.

The Germans knew a starving man
needed more than soup and more than bread
but still they stood and watched.

A Story My Mother Heard in the Slave Labor Camp

They took me from my children, three little ones.

They said the children would be useless in the camps in Germany.
They were too young to do anything but cry for food.

I begged the soldiers to let me take them with me. I said I'd care for
them and do the work both. I even dropped on my knees and wept,
clung to their boots, but they said no.

I asked them who would feed them, and they said surely a neighbor
would.

I couldn't stop weeping, and they said if I didn't, they would shoot the
children.

So I left them behind in Dębno.

The Work My Father Did in Germany

He lifts the shovel, sees the dirt,
the clods still heavy with snow,
and knows that this will always
be his life, one shovel and then
another shovel until his arms
are shaking. He never knows

what the guards will say to him.
Maybe they'll ask him for a song
he knew in Poland that he sang
while leading the steaming cows
into the woods early in the spring.
And he will smile and sing

and ask them if they'd like another.
Or maybe they will tell him
he is a fool and his mother
a pig the farm boys fuck
when their own hands are weak
from pulling on their sore meat.

And my father will shovel
in terror and think of the words
he will not say: Sirs, we are all
brothers, and if this war ever ends,
please, never tell your children
what you've done to me today.

A Life Story

She was born
in a concentration camp
in 1944. She was one pound
eight ounces. She was
a leaf of grass. She was lovely.

She was born dreaming
her mother's dream
of flying like a robin
through the sky and eating
everything that was pure
and good and golden.

And then the women guards
smashed her into the wall
and wrapped her in newspaper
and threw her in the garbage
with the others.

My Father Tells a Story

My friend Jasiu was an artist in Wilno
before the war. He would paint pictures
of young women in dresses made of roses
and yellow flowers no one had ever seen.

In the camp he would push a stick
through the dust and sketch your face
give you eyes like Charlie Chaplin
or a funny stomach like Oliver Hardy.

Jasiu told me of the women he knew
before the war, of making love in blue rooms
after a dessert of marzipan on silver plates,
then going into the dark, wet park

And making love again in the half shelter
of a band shell or kiosk. Near the end
he told me he had the French disease,
and when I said I didn't understand

he pointed down to his thing there
and asked me what he should do.
He was a good friend, and I looked him
in the eye and said, "Go to the Elbe

And drown yourself." He laughed and went
to Stefan Czernak who said, "Go to the Germans
And tell them what you did." The Germans asked,
"Who was the woman you made love to?"

He told them, and they beat her with clubs
and killed her and they beat him too,
and castrated him, and killed him.

Brief History of a Mother's Sorrow

Sorrow is the gift
God gives to teach us
what won't last,
what will fall and be left
on the side of the road
by the mother lost
among refugees.

Sorrow teaches her
the value of screaming.

It will last longer
than bronze shoes,
longer than her baby's
photograph.

Nothing else she loved
is left. The home in Poland
God bestowed? The husband
whose love was worth so much?
The baby?

The gift of everything is lost,
the way a penny is lost
in the dirt around her.

All that's left
is the road she stands on—
that and the sorrow
He bestowed, the scream
that ends in screaming.

.

My Father's Teeth

Dying on this wind-still February morning
he looks at the teeth in his hands,
yellow, shrunken, his own, pulled by a guard
for some stupid infraction: smiling
at the beets, pissing out of turn,
dreaming of the way his mother spoke of mares
sleeping beneath the trees in the field

He wonders, how can he use them: bead them
for a rosary, sell them for souvenirs?
He knows God has answered all the prayers
He will, and tired of the camps even He
no longer looks for Buchenwald on the maps

The Forests of Katyń

There are no Great Walls there,
No Towers leaning or not leaning
Declaring some king's success
Or mocking another's failure,
No gleaming Duomo where you can
Pray for forgiveness or watch
The cycle of shadows play
Through the coolness of the day.

And soon not even the names
Of those who died will be remembered
(Names like Skrzypiński, Chmura,
Or Anthony Milczarek).
Their harsh voices and tearing courage
Are already lost in the wind.

But their true monuments
Will always be there, in the dust
And the gray ashes and the mounds
Settling on the bodies over which
No words were ever spoken
And no tears shed by a crying mother
Or a trembling sister.

The Third Winter of War: Buchenwald

Prologue:
His hands are cut into pieces,
each piece small, pebble size.

If you are hungry at night,
You'll put a piece in your mouth.

I.

He dreams about fires and bricks,
a church he saw in Warsaw
after the bombers pulled it apart
and broke it up, and smashed it
and left it bleeding and praying
for death the way a woman
in labor will pray when she knows
nothing will save the baby
waiting in her womb to be born.

II.

Sometimes at night, the guards tell him
to milk the cows. He smiles and nods.

The cow's hair is soft, like his mother's,
and warm as a stove steaming on a gray
winter morning.

     The mud and shit
around the cows are warm too.

In the dark, he raises his cupped hands,
drinks the milk, and knows there'll be more,
and knows too the guards will club him
when they smell the milk on his lips.

III.

He is swimming in a dark river.

Above his head there is a moon
as big as a theater he once saw
in Magdeburg, but there is no light.

The moon is a bright place in the sky
but none of the light falls on him
or his journey's path.

     He remembers
he cannot swim and begins falling
without struggling, deeper and deeper
into the black water.

     Nothing
will save him. He knows this and wakes
waiting to dream of the river's bottom.

IV.

The bricks of the burning city are hot.
He doesn't have to touch them to know this.
Everywhere he looks, people stand away
from the bricks, stand with their hands raised

as if to keep the city's death at bay.
Even where the dying shout and plead
under the hot bricks, people stand this way.
They stand in the middle of the street.

It's not important who is under the bricks.
It could be a soldier or a child, a mother
or one of the other slaves forced like him to dig
under the bricks for the living and the dead.

The people don't want to know who is under
the hot bricks. When a thing is truly bad,
you can do nothing to change it. You must
stand away from it—hands raised.

V.

He feels trees are growing in him,
their roots hardening into bone,
the bone growing into stone,
the stone hardening into iron,

and the iron in turn hardening
into steel and more sorrow.

What is the blood in his heart?

VI.

Beyond the field and the guards,
he sees a witch in the pine trees
dancing in rags, the snow a veil,

the witch twirling like a girl
in a spring world of greens and blues
so rich not even a holy man

would turn away, a witch twirling
her arms above her head, her breasts
fat as pillows, warm as fresh milk,

singing a child's song about cows
coming home from the happy fields
and the pretty girls who lead them,

singing a song to Jesus and Mary
His mother who hears our prayers
and beseeches Him to hear them too.

VII.

He remembers a movie he once saw
when he escaped from the camp.

In it, one of the heroes is a fat man,
the other skinny. On a boat lost at sea,
they look at each other in hunger and cry.

Then fatty smiles, and skinny cries harder.

VIII.

He dreams he's one of the Boy Scouts
of Katowice, forced to jump
by the Germans from the tower
in the park. He falls screaming.

His courage will not give him wings.

His dead mother watches and cries.
Waking, he remembers her love
for him and how he cried
when she died in the winter.

Her love couldn't give her wings.

IX.

He is as hungry as a dog in winter
in a forest filled with so much snow
that all the woodsmen and their wives
and children have fled to the village.

Only the tips of the highest pine trees
peek out, their needles pointed east
ready for spring's first light to shine.

X.

He dreams about men whose hands
change color, from yellow and black,
to white and green, the men staring
at their rainbow hands and whistling
like boys calling dogs.

       The change
doesn't frighten them, but they worry
about what their fathers and mothers
will say when they come home,
old with hands like rainbows.

XI.

He lies on a shelf at night and thinks
of milk and oranges, sausage
and chicken breasts, his mother's bread,
brown and warm, boiled dumplings
filled with sauerkraut, dumplings
filled with soft cheese, dumplings
filled with plums and sweet cherries,
and all of them pitted and perfect.

He knows he never again has to worry
about breaking his teeth on the pits.

His teeth were left in the frozen mud
where the guard hit him with the club.

XII.

He dreams dogs change into men
and sit at a table to discuss the war,
why it began and how it will end.

He wants to ask the dogs a question
but they can't understand his howling.

XIII.

Through the nearest window
he stares at the sky and thinks
of his dead father and mother,
his dead sister and brother,

his dead aunt and dead uncle,
his dead friend Jasiu, and the boy
whose name he didn't know
who died in his arms, and all

the others who wait for him
like the first light of the sun
and the work he has to do
when the sun wakes him.

He hates no one, not God,
not the dead who come to him,
not the Germans who caught him,
not even himself for being alive.

He is a man held together
with stitches he laced himself.

XIV.

Beneath the skin on his arms,
he sees stones growing, pressing
against his skin, trying to burst through.

He pushes them down, but the pain
in his arms is terrible, violent,
a burning no one can stop.

Crying like a fool, he tries
to pull the stones out, digs his fingers
deeper into his bones for the stones
that pull deeper and deeper down.

XV.

He dreams a comedy—men lifting
heavy wooden trunks onto a cart
and slipping in manure, rising
again and then slipping again.

This goes on until their faces,
hands and clothes are covered
in brown and green and yellow.

He laughs until someone kicks him.

XVI.

His urine is soapy, the color
of wheat, and there is always pain
when he pees.

    He watches it like
a man on an island watches the tides.

XVII.

He wakes in the night in the barracks,
his sweat cold among the dying.

He knows there are thieves all around
who will steal his wooden shoes
and the belt that keeps his pants up
and the bread he hides at his groin.

These thieves are like his brothers,
but at night loneliness and sorrow
will turn your brother against you.

XVIII.

He dreams about men becoming
talking animals, dogs and horses,
cows and lions, and even creatures
he's never seen but only heard of,
the elephant and the gorilla,
the hippopotamus and the zebra.

He dreams again his hands are cut
to pieces. He dreams he is falling.
He dreams he is an old woman
eating the fingers of a young boy
who died when his horse reared
up crazily and crushed him.

He dreams of women copulating
with corpses, of dogs licking his fingers,
of soldiers spreading manure
around the red and white roses
beside the church in his village.

He dreams he swims in a river
he can't escape. It is the blood
of the devil, thick and dark
and acid to the tongue.

XIX.

Working among the bricks, lifting
them in his hands and throwing them
into the wooden cart behind him,
his body first feels hot and then
cold with the sickness and the snow.

He fears his bones will freeze and crack
the way the limbs of a tree will crack
when winter is so hard it can kill
a dog, and even kill a man.

XX.

The Germans are pulling him apart
and rushing him to the furnace.

They are like devils and the heat
burns the hair from his face.

He struggles but they beat him
with black snaking whips.

     The wind
around his head swirls with the sound
of the whipping and the cutting.

XXI.

He dreams he is in a blue house
that collapses every night
as if the strongest wind God
ever imagined sought out
this very house every night
and pulled its iron nails loose.

XXII.

He recalls talking with two priests
when he was just a boy. They walked
with him among the pines and held
his hands gently, told him, "There's hope

but there is also waiting. Hope
will come but waiting is the road
upon which it travels and it travels
so slowly. Till then, remember

the faith you were born to, no matter
what you are told and no matter
how much life seems to fail you,
no matter how much you fail life."

XXIII.

This is the winter that will not end,
the winter that leaves the cows frozen
in the snow, frozen in the smell
of swirling cordite from the shells—

A winter that will never end.

XXIV.

My father is the corpse without lips
or the desire to lick its lips.

He is the corpse that doesn't envy
the sparrows or the pigeons,
or the horses or cows that stand
around waiting for men to beat them
across the flanks when they're angry
or across the eyes and mouth
when the men are truly mad.

He is the corpse that has made
its journey and now waits only
for the slumber promised by God
in the Bible and other books that lie.

Epilogue:

*If he plants his cut-off hands in the ground
will they take root, bring him the promise
of his mother and father, will a stem
grow from his wrist, leaves from his fingers,*

*will these be his children, will he know
how to water them, will his water be
enough to bring them the love they'll seek
as they uncurl like roses before the spring sun,*

*will his tears be the holy, saving water,
or will they be a blasphemy against
his Blessed Lord, just the bitterness
of a cow disappointed with its field?*

My Mother's Dreams in Wartime

The world burns before our eyes,
and the smell of everything red
is on our skin.

We wait in line for bread
that never comes. We speak
to strangers thinking they will
tell us where our lives are.

We pray in the barracks
and the fields for the miracle
of hope.

What My Father Knows About Killing

My father knows men and animals
do not die the same way. A man
will kill a horse or a cow or a pig
with respect he'll never show a man.

Killing a pig, a man will steady it,
prepare it for the single killing blow,
work to make its suffering quick
if not instant, a poised hammer
ready to strike down in such a way
the pig won't see it or hear it,
will hardly feel it on the back
of its head in that one sure spot
that will end it before it knows it.

My father knows that isn't the way
men kill each other. He has seen
men crucified and hung, castrated
and frozen to death, women raped
and beaten and shot, their breasts
torn apart by bayonets, their babies
thrown and scattered in the air like sand.

He says that suffering is the sauce
we reserve for men and women.

Today the Gypsies Are Burning

Their dying is something fierce,
like a blizzard wind, like wolves
startled into anger and rage
by the death of one of their own.

Their singing rises in the wind,
their red and orange scarves
and sparrow shawls swirling
in a maelstrom of gasoline flames.

Death cannot hold them.

These pilgrims need no God
to save them, no coin to buy them free,
no gray statue on the cusp of time.

The wind's their mother, their home.

Temptation in the Desert

If a German soldier comes to you
and asks you to shoot the man
next to you because that man
isn't even bones in his striped suit,

tell the soldier, "No, you're the devil,
and though you offer me the cities
of the world and all their soft women
and bread, I won't shoot this man
though he is dead as I am dead.

We are brothers in death, and brothers
in death don't torment each other
no matter what the prize, no matter
that death is the only prize left."

Photos of Dead Mothers

They are simple as arithmetic. One minus one
is nothing. You see this in their blind, dumb eyes,
the twist of their bodies lying in the mud,
the truth of their silence. There is nothing
to tell one mother from another. They are dead.

No one has anything to grieve or remember.

The mouth cracked open tells you nothing
about her first child, or that day in the church
that meant so much, or the happy time she stood
before the Christmas tree knowing how much
her daughter would love the light blue pitcher
she gave her, no matter how little it cost.

The Bombing of Magdeburg

My father digs for the living
in the cellar. The smell

of death doubling and tripling,
like some crazy, invisible

dough that keeps rising
in his stomach, a hot nausea

he can't vomit up.

Somewhere beneath this flood of bricks
a German woman cries suddenly,

her cry a single, long strand
of fear that threads

through the smoke
and swirling dust.

He digs faster.

Pietà in a Bombed Church, Magdeburg

My father remembers the church at midnight,
the church at dawn, altars and crosses
in shadows, a statue of a mother holding
the body of the man who was her son,
his wounds chiseled deep and cold, like mouths
hardened into stone by pain and death.

The mother and son are the color of clay
before it hardens in the kiln, the color
of the body seen on the doctor's table
or left dying in a field by soldiers.
The son looks at her face, as if he can't
turn away from her sorrow, a sorrow
she shows even in the way she holds
her head. It's clear to my father she knows
pain and how pain is like the night that never
seems to end, but sometimes finally does,
suddenly like the first of winter's frosts.

My father's memories of his own mother
are few but holy: her standing near the stove,
her sitting in the doorway with the warmth
of the sun on her face. Her hand holding
his while she probes his palm with a needle
to get the sliver out, his palm swollen,
a blister filled with pus where the sliver
waits for her needle. He feared the pain
the needle would bring, and there was pain
when she probed, and pain when she withdrew
the sliver, and pain when she pressed the fire
to his palm to burn the wound clean of poison,
but he knew she wouldn't hurt him and the pain
would be there only for a minute, and then
it would stop the greater pain inside it.

Awake already, he doesn't open his eyes.
The room's filled with the sounds of hungry men
sleeping, their groans and the waking whispers
that might be threats or prayers. Enslaved men
never sleep soundly. They dream of sorrow
and food, and the distance between them
and the ones they love, the mothers who wait
beside stoves, the fathers who sleep in their graves.

His Dead Eye

My father didn't know why he didn't die
when they clubbed him for eating the soup.

For a long time he wasn't there or anywhere,
and when he came to, his left eye was dead,
dead and open and would always stay open,
with a scar running curved and deep
from this left eye to a place above his ear.

Sometimes at night, pain would shake him awake,
and he would pray to Jesus through his fear
until he fell asleep. Sometimes, he felt the pain
during the day too, and he'd grow angry
with the men and women in the labor camp
who were like his brothers and sisters
over things they all knew didn't matter,
like shoeing a horse or clearing bricks
or bracing a barn's collapsing wall.

Later in Chicago looking for work
in some factory on Armitage Street,
my father wasn't hired once because the boss
couldn't face the scar and the dead, staring eye.

When my father died the undertaker fixed
the scar with putty and sewed the eye shut.

Worthless

My mother looks at herself
in her dress and striped coat
and knows she is who she is—
bones and skin, and the war
has always been here with her,

like an older brother, not mean
or evil but hard, never soft, teaching
hesitance and patience, teaching her
not to put her hand out to take
the cup of water or touch the bread.

It has always been this way
and will always be this way.
War has no beginning, no end.
War is the god who breeds and kills.

War and Peace

War will kill you
and leave you
cold in the street
or in the fields,
broken in the rubble
of bombed buildings

But don't worry:
peace will come
and bury you
and sit over you
weeping like your mother,
praying for you,
pleading for your return

She'll whisper to you
like when you were
a boy in the stream
washing your hands and face
before breakfast

She will weep until
God brings a miracle:
you risen again
in golden rays
and singing birds

and then war
will return
and kill you

In the Spring the War Ended

For a long time the war was not in the camps.
My father worked in the fields and listened
to the wind moving the grain, or a guard
shouting a command far off, or a man dying.

But in the fall, my father heard the rumbling
whisper of American planes, so high, like
angels, cutting through the sky, a thunder
even God in Heaven would have to listen to.

At last, one day he knew the war was there.
In the door of the barracks stood a soldier,
an American, short like a boy and frightened,
and my father marveled at the miracle of his youth

and took his hands and embraced him and told him
he loved him and his mother and father,
and he would pray for all his children
and even forgive him the sin of taking so long.

EPILOGUE

The Story Behind the Poems

"My Mother Was 19"—one of the first poems in Book III—is about what happened the day the Germans came to my mother's farm in Poland and killed much of her family. It wasn't an easy poem to write. I had been trying to write this poem for about thirty years.

How do you talk about the women in your family being brutalized, your grandmother and your aunt murdered, your aunt's baby getting kicked to death? Your mother being raped? Her escape from the home where this happened? The way this all affected her?

For a long time, I couldn't write about it because I didn't know enough about it. My mother wouldn't talk about it. If I asked her to tell me about what happened, she'd just wave me away saying, "If they give you bread, you eat it. If they beat you, you run away." And when my dad talked about what happened when the Germans came, it was mainly whispers and bits of information that I would have to try to piece together. I think he was afraid to tell the story because he didn't want to burden me with the terror my mom experienced.

So when I first started writing about what happened to my parents, the poems that came out mainly came from what my dad told me. They were about everything that happened except for what happened. I wrote about the dry summer at the start of the war, the boxcars the Germans put my mom on, the landscape she passed through on the train trip to the slave labor camps in Germany, the work she did in those camps, and her liberation at the end of the war. I even wrote a poem called "Here's What My Mother Won't Talk About," but it too was a poem that didn't talk about what happened.

This all changed when these poems were translated and published in Poland under the title *Język mułów i inne wiersze (Language of Mules and Other Verses)*. My mom was in her late seventies then, and up to this point, I had been occasionally showing her my poems about her and my dad, but she couldn't read the poems because they were in English. So when she saw the poems she would say, "Hmm, that's interesting" and move on.

This changed when I showed her my poems in a Polish edition.

She read them.

She sat right down and read about ten of the poems right there. I couldn't believe it. She was actually reading my poems. You can imagine what was going through my head. Then she looked at me and said, "That's not how it was."

She started talking then about what had happened when the Germans came to her home and what happened after the killing, her capture, her grief, and the years of misery in the slave labor camps in Germany. My mom was filling in the bits that my father left out or thought I wasn't ready to hear.

My mom and I kept up this conversation until she died four years later. A lot of times I would go to see her, and she would ask me to take out a pen and some paper because she remembered something else she wanted to say about her years under the Germans.

It wasn't always easy listening to these stories. Sometimes, my mother would stop herself in the middle of a story and tell me she couldn't finish it because "even though you are a grown man and a teacher," there were things that happened that she couldn't tell me.

There were other times when I had to ask my mother not to tell me any more because there were things she was telling me that I did not want to hear. I remember one of the last conversations she and I had about the war. She was 83 years old and dying of all the things she was dying from, and we were sitting in her living room in the evening in Sun City, Arizona, and she was telling me about the war. This time, she was telling me about what it was like just before liberation. She was telling me what the German soldiers were doing to the girls in the camps. One terrible thing after another. And I looked up and saw that she was about to tell me something so terrible that it would just about be the worst thing I'd ever heard, the last flash and stroke of lightning, and I said to her, "Mom, I don't want to hear it."

And she said, "I'm going to tell you. You want to know what it was like, and I'm going to tell you."

And I said, "Please don't tell me."

And she said, "I'm going to tell you," and I said, "If you do, I'll leave and not come back. I'll stand up and leave and you won't see me again."

And she said, "Okay, you're 58 years old and still a baby, so I won't tell you."

In Heaven

I will sit around the table
eating poppy-seed cake
and drinking coffee
with my mom and dad

They will tell me all the things
they were afraid or forgot to tell me
when they were alive

The first will be about this moment,
this place, this death, the world they
couldn't imagine here above the clouds,
different from the stories the priests told

Then they will tell me everything else:
Maybe my mom and dad will say
it was fear that kept them silent
or kept them from telling the truth to me.
Nothing they had seen in life prepared
them for what they would see in the camps,
not the cows dying suddenly in the fields
nor their grandmothers suffering in their
beds beneath the pictures of Jesus
with his open heart, its red rays radiating out
into the room but giving
no warmth or true comfort

But this will take only a moment
—real explanations never take longer
than that—and then they will turn
to the only questions that really matter
to the living and the dead.

Was the road hard?
Did you miss us?

APPENDIX

"Red Poppies on Monte Cassino"

The Battle of Monte Cassino was one of the longest and most ferocious battles of World War II. For five months, Allied attempts to advance in Italy were blocked by the Germans, who commanded the terrain from their mountain stronghold atop Monte Cassino.

Finally, in May 1944, the Polish Second Corps succeeded in taking Monte Cassino—after three prior attempts by other Allied forces had failed. With their victory, the Poles opened the road to Rome for the Allies, but the cost in Polish dead and wounded was steep.

The land was blanketed with red poppies in May. A Polish soldier, Feliks Konarski, wrote a poem that has become one of the best-known songs in Poland, and is referred to in three of the poems in this book.

"Czerwone maki na Monte Cassino"

Czerwone maki na Monte Cassino
Zamiast rosy piły polską krew...
Po tych makach szedł żołnierz i ginął,
Lecz od śmierci silniejszy był gniew!
Przejdą lata i wieki przeminą,
Pozostaną ślady dawnych dni!...
I tylko maki na Monte Cassino
Czerwieńsze będą, bo z polskiej wzrosną krwi.

"Red Poppies on Monte Cassino"

Red poppies on Monte Cassino,
Instead of dew, drank Polish blood...
Through these poppies Polish soldiers marched and died,
Their anger stronger than death!
Years will pass and ages will roll,
But traces of bygone battles will linger...
And the poppies on Monte Cassino
Will glow the reddest, having drunk the blood of Poles.

ACKNOWLEDGMENTS

This book would not be this book without the encouragement, generosity, diligence, and creativity of my publisher and editor Terry Tegnazian. She made every page better, closer to my vision of what my parents would have wanted to read and see.

John Guzlowski

Some of the poems and prose pieces included in *Echoes of Tattered Tongues: Memory Unfolded* have appeared in the following journals and books (in some cases, in an earlier form and/or under a different title):

Poetry Journals (print and/or online):
53 Fragments Project: "The Day I Was Born in the Refugee Camp: Prose Poem"
Akcent: "My Father's Teeth"
Atticus Review: "Brief History of Sorrow"
Chattahoochee Review: "The Evil that Men Do"; "My Mother Was 19"
Connecticut River Review: "Today the Gypsies are Burning"; "Polack Joe Tells His Story"; "All the Clichés about Poverty are True"
Consequence Magazine: "War and Peace"
Cosmopolitan Review: "Dumb Polacks"; "Kitchen Polish"; "Second Language Acquisition"
Crab Orchard Review: "Hunger in the Labor Camps"
Escape into Life: "Life Story"
Outside in Literary and Travel Magazine: "Promised Land"
Prism: An Interdisciplinary Journal for Holocaust Educators: "My Father's First Day in America"
Redux: A Literary Journal: "The Story Behind the Poems"
SGI Quarterly: "Happy Places"

Spoon River Poetry Review: "Temptation in the Desert"; "Kitchen Polish"; "German Soldiers Moving East"

War, Literature & the Arts: "My Mother Tells Me How She Met My Father: Prose Poem"; "Fear"; "Landscape with Dead Horses"; "Photos of Dead Mothers"

Anthologies (print):

Chopin with Cherries (Moonrise Press, 2010): "A Good Death"

Longman Academic Reading Series 5 Student Book (Pearson Education ESL, 2013): "Wooden Trunk from Buchenwald"

Books (print):

Language of Mules (DP Press, 1999): "Windows Without Scars"; "A Good Death"; "Lessons"; "Displaced Persons"; "My Mother's Sister After the War"; "His Mother Asks Him to Forget the War"; "Pigeons"; "Cross of Polish Wood"; "Forests of Katyn"; "Dreams of Poland, September 1939"; "My Grandparents"

Lightning and Ashes (Steel Toe Books, 2007): "My Mother Prays for Death"; "My Mother Talks About the Slave Labor Camps"; "My Mother's Optimism"; "Dying in a Blue Room in Arizona"; "Why My Mother Stayed with My Father"; "My Mother Reads My Poem 'Cattle Train to Magdeburg' "; "Work and Death"; "My Father Dying"; "What My Father Believed"; "Looking for Work in America"; "A Letter to My Mother from Poland, October 4, 1952"; "Stories My Sister Danusha Told Me"; "Dumb Polacks"; "Whistling"; "A Young Soldier from Czestochowa"; "Fussy Eaters"; "Danusha"; "Chores"; "Poland"; "My Father's Prayer"; "Here's What My Mother Won't Talk About"; "There Were No Miracles"; "Soldiers Come to My Mother's Village"; "Cattle Train to Magdeburg"; "My Father Talks about the Boxcars"; "Grief"; "Hunger in the Labor Camps"; "The Work My Father Did in Germany"; "My Father Tells a Story"; "The Beets"; "Third Winter of War: Buchenwald"; "Worthless"; "Pieta in a Bombed Church: Magdeburg"; "His Dead Eye"; "In the Spring the War Ended"

Third Winter of War: Buchenwald (Finishing Line Press, 2007): "Third Winter of War: Buchenwald"

AUTHOR BIO

Over a writing career that spans more than 40 years, **John Z. Guzlowski** has amassed a significant body of published work in a wide range of genres: poetry, prose, literary criticism, reviews, fiction and nonfiction.

 His poems and stories have appeared in such national journals as *North American Review, Ontario Review, Rattle, Chattahoochee Review, Atlanta Review, Nimrod, Crab Orchard Review, Marge, Poetry East, Vocabula Review.* He was the featured poet in the 2007 edition of *Spoon River Poetry Review.* Garrison Keillor read Guzlowski's poem "What My Father Believed" on his program *The Writers Almanac.*

Critical essays by Guzlowski about contemporary American, Polish, and Jewish authors can be found in such journals as *Modern Fiction Studies, Polish Review, Shofar, Polish American Studies, Critique: Studies in Contemporary Fiction,* and *Studies in Jewish American Literature.*

His previously published books include *Language of Mules* (DP Press), *Język mułów i inne wiersze* (Biblioteka Śląska), *Lightning and Ashes* (Steel Toe Books), *Third Winter of War: Buchenwald* (Finishing Line Press), and *Suitcase Charlie* (White Stag/Ravenswood). Guzlowski's work has also been included in anthologies such as *Blood to Remember: American Poets on the Holocaust* (Time Being Books), *Chopin with Cherries* (Moonrise Press), *Common Boundary: Stories of Immigration* (Editions Bibliotekos), and *Longman Academic Reading Series 5 Student Book* (Pearson Education ESL).

Winner of the Illinois Arts Council's $7,500 Award for Poetry, Guzlowski has also been short-listed for the Bakeless Award and

Eric Hoffer Award, and nominated for the Pulitzer Prize and four Pushcart Prizes. He has been honored by the Georgia State Commission on the Holocaust for his work.

In reviewing Guzlowski's book *Language of Mules*, Nobel Laureate Czesław Miłosz wrote, "Exceptional...even astonished me...reveals an enormous ability for grasping reality."

Born in a refugee camp in Germany after World War II, Guzlowski came to America with his family as a Displaced Person in 1951. His parents had been Polish slave laborers in Nazi Germany during the war. Growing up in the tough immigrant neighborhoods around Humboldt Park in Chicago, he met hardware-store clerks with Auschwitz tattoos on their wrists, Polish cavalry officers who still mourned for their dead horses, and women who had walked from Siberia to Iran to escape the Russians. In much of his work, Guzlowski remembers and honors the experiences and ultimate strength of these voiceless survivors.

Guzlowski received his B.A. in English Literature from the University of Illinois, Chicago, and his M.A. and Ph.D. in English from Purdue University. He is Professor Emeritus of English Literature at Eastern Illinois University, and currently lives in Lynchburg, Virginia.

DISCUSSION QUESTIONS

1. In *Echoes of Tattered Tongues: Memory Unfolded*, the author John Guzlowski tells his family's story primarily through poems. He could have written the same story entirely as a prose narrative. How does his choice of medium impact your perception of the story? Do you find the use of poetry more or less powerful than a straightforward prose narrative would have been? Why?

2. Another technique used by the author is to tell the story backwards in time. Do you think this is more effective or less effective than telling the story in chronological order? Why?

3. In what ways are the title *Echoes of Tattered Tongues*, and subtitle *Memory Unfolded*, appropriate for this book?

4. In the opening prose piece of Book I—Half a Century Later, entitled "The Wooden Trunk," the author describes the wooden trunk made by his father from the walls of their refugee-camp barracks, in which the family brought their meager possessions to America. His parents carried that trunk with them in every move they made throughout the rest of their lives in America, even when they left behind other furniture. Why do you think his parents did that? Is it significant that they eventually painted and papered over the trunk?

5. After his mother's death, the author decided to sell the wooden trunk. What did that trunk mean to the author? Was he right in deciding not to keep it? What would you have done?

6. If you were forced to move to a new land and allowed to take only one trunk of possessions for your entire family, what would you put in that trunk?

7. Most people are aware of how the Germans targeted Jews for extinction during World War II, now commonly referred to as the Holocaust. Before reading *Echoes of Tattered Tongues*, were you aware that Christian civilians such as the author's parents were also rounded up by the Germans and sent to concentration camps, where they were forced to work as slave laborers with little chance of survival? How does this affect your understanding of what was at stake in World War II?

8. Shortly before invading Poland to begin World War II, Hitler reportedly commanded his forces "to kill without pity or mercy, all men, women, and children of Polish descent or language." Would you classify this campaign against all Poles as part of the Holocaust? Why or why not?

9. In Book I, we see the author's parents near the end of their lives. What are their views on life, aging and dying? How are they similar? How are they different? How would you describe the author's relationship with his parents in Book I?

10. In the introductory section of Book II—Refugees, the author includes a prose piece called "The Happy Times and Places." What are those happy times and places like? Why do you think the author feels he needs to include them at the start of Book II? What are your memories of "happy times and places" while you were growing up? How do they compare to the author's?

11. The neighborhood in Chicago where the author's family settled was populated by many immigrants and refugees. We see glimpses of this neighborhood in several of the poems, especially those in the "Friends in America" series. What sense of the lives of these other immigrants does the author give us in this section?

12. Recently, we hear a lot about PTSD (post-traumatic stress disorder) in connection with military veterans returning from combat. The author's parents were Polish peasants—civilians, not soldiers. Nevertheless, what signs of PTSD do you see in the author's parents? How about in some of their neighbors described in Book II?

13. The author's parents came from different parts of Poland (his father, from the northwest; his mother, from the southeast), were sent to different concentration camps, did not meet until after the war, and of course were of different sexes. What things do each of them remember about the war? How did their wartime experiences differ? How were they similar?

14. After the war, how did each parent deal with the trauma he or she had experienced during the war?

15. What is the relationship between the author's parents like? Should they have gotten divorced? Why didn't they?

16. How do his parents' wartime experiences affect the author and his sister Danusia? Describe both the short-term and long-term impacts.

17. The author doesn't say much about what the refugee camps in Germany were like after the war, but he does drop some hints. How does he describe them?

18. What is America like for the new immigrants? What kind of experiences does the author talk about? How do the experiences of the author and his sister, who were children, compare to their parents' experiences as new immigrants?

19. As the author and his sister grow up, they reject their immigrant background and their "old-world" parents in order to become "American." Do you think this is a typical dynamic in immigrant families? As the author and his sister mature into adults, does their relationship with their parents and their own immigrant past evolve, and if so, how? If you, or any of your family or friends, are immigrants, how does that experience compare to the experiences of the author's family?

20. When we think of immigrants and refugees, we tend to focus on their experiences in the new country, but often their own thoughts are on the people they left behind in the old country. What does the author tell us about the lives of those who were left behind?

21. In the introductory section of Book III—War, the author begins with two poems ("Landscape with Dead Horses" and "Fear") and a prose piece called "September 1, 1939: The Day World War II Began." How does this introduction prepare us for the works that follow?

22. In the two poems "My Mother Before the War" and "My Father Before the War," the author quickly sketches a portrait of prewar Poland. What are his parents' lives like during peacetime? What memories of prewar life did each parent carry with them? What part, if any, do these memories play during and after the war?

23. In a series of poems under the title "The German Soldiers" that appears early in Book III, the author switches our point of view to the invading German soldiers. What is the war like for these men?

24. In the poem "Fear," the author suggests that what lingers after the war, after a traumatic experience, is a sense of fear. Think back to the poems you read in Books I and II. Was there fear expressed in those poems?

25. In the long poem "Third Winter of War: Buchenwald," the author uses a surrealistic approach, mixing dreams and impressionistic realism, to convey a sense of the horrors of his father's experience.

How effective is this technique compared to the more graphic poems and prose pieces?

26. A number of poems make mention of God. How does each parent's image of God change as a result of their wartime experiences? How do they differ from each other? What is the author's image of God? How does this compare with your image of God?

27. What poems or prose pieces affected you most strongly, and why?

28. What do you think the author wants you to carry away from this book?

Also from Aquila Polonica Publishing...

303 Squadron: The Legendary Battle of Britain Fighter Squadron

by **Arkady Fiedler**, Translated by Jarek Garlinski
- Hardcover: 978-1-60772-004-1 ($27.95)
  Trade Paperback: 978-1-60772-005-8 ($21.95)
- 368 pages. Nearly 200 black and white photos, maps and illustrations; contextualizing historical material; nine appendices.
- Nonfiction.
- A Selection of the **History Book Club** and the **Military Book Club**.
- **Winner of 2011 Benjamin Franklin GOLD Award for History and SILVER Award for Interior Design.**

Thrilling action story of the famous squadron of Polish fighter pilots whose superb aerial skills helped save Britain during its most desperate hours. They were the highest-scoring Allied fighter squadron in the entire Battle of Britain—downing three times the average RAF squadron with one-third the losses. Underdog heroes who rose to defend against the deadly German Luftwaffe attacks, the pilots of 303 Squadron were lionized by the British press, congratulated by the King, and adored by the British public.

"About as exciting as it gets...a must-read." — *The Washington Times*

The Auschwitz Volunteer: Beyond Bravery

by **Captain Witold Pilecki**
Translated by Jarek Garlinski
Introduction by Norman Davies
Foreword by Rabbi Michael Schudrich, Chief Rabbi of Poland
- Hardcover: 978-1-60772-009-6 ($42.95)
  Trade Paperback: 978-1-60772-010-2 ($34.95)
  Ebook: 978-1-60772-014-0 ($19.99)
  Audiobook: Audible.com and Brilliance Audio
- 460 pages. More than 80 black and white photos, maps and illustrations; contextualizing historical material; four appendices; Discussion Questions; Index.
- Nonfiction.
- A Featured Selection of the **History Book Club**; a Selection of the **Book-of-the-Month Club** and the **Military Book Club**.

- Winner of the 2012 PROSE Award for Biography & Autobiography; winner of the 2013 Benjamin Franklin SILVER Award for Autobiography/Memoir.

In one of the most heroic acts of WWII, Pilecki volunteered for an almost certainly suicidal undercover mission: get himself arrested and sent to Auschwitz as a prisoner in order to smuggle out intelligence about the camp and build a resistance organization among the prisoners. His clandestine reports from Auschwitz were among the first to reach the Allies, beginning in early 1941. He accomplished his mission, barely surviving nearly three years before escaping. Pilecki's most comprehensive eyewitness report on his mission is published here in English for the first time.

"A historical document of the greatest importance."
— *The New York Times*, Editors' Choice

The Color of Courage—A Boy at War: The World War II Diary of Julian Kulski
by Julian Kulski
Foreword by Lech Wałęsa, Nobel Peace Prize Laureate
Introduction by Rabbi Michael Schudrich, Chief Rabbi of Poland

- Hardcover: 978-1-60772-015-7 ($29.95)
  Trade Paperback: 978-1-60772-016-4 ($19.95)
- 496 pages. More than 150 black and white photos, maps and illustrations; 11 groundbreaking Digital Extras; contextualizing historical material; two appendices;

Discussion Questions; Index. Educators' Guide correlated to Common Core Standards, Grades 9–12, available free online.
- Nonfiction.
- A Selection of the **History Book Club** and the **Military Book Club.**
- Winner of 2015 Benjamin Franklin GOLD Award for Interior Design and SILVER for Autobiography/Memoir.
- Finalist, *Foreword Reviews* IndieFab BOOK OF THE YEAR Award.

This remarkable diary follows Kulski, a 10-year-old Boy Scout when WWII begins, as he is recruited into the clandestine Polish Underground Army by his Scoutmaster, undertakes a secret mission into Warsaw Ghetto, is captured by the Gestapo, sentenced to Auschwitz, rescued, fights in the Warsaw Uprising and ends as a 16-year-old German POW, risking a dash for freedom onto an American truck instead of waiting for "liberation" by the Soviets.

"Absorbing, inspiring, and tragic." — *Publishers Weekly*

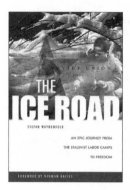

The Ice Road: An Epic Journey from the Stalinist Labor Camps to Freedom
by Stefan Waydenfeld
Foreword by Norman Davies
- Hardcover: 978-1-60772-002-7 ($28.95)
  Trade Paperback: 978-1-60772-003-4 ($18.95)
  Ebook: 978-1-60772-017-1 ($12.99)
  Audiobook: Audible.com
- 400 pages. More than 70 black and white photos, maps and illustrations; contextualizing historical material; author interview; Reading Group Guide.
- Nonfiction.

- A Selection of the **History Book Club** and the **Military Book Club.**
- **Winner of 2011 Benjamin Franklin SILVER Award for Autobiography/Memoir.**

Fourteen years old when WWII began, Stefan Waydenfeld and his family were deported by cattle car in 1940 from Poland to a forced labor camp in the frozen wastes of the Russian arctic north. Coming of age was never so dangerous—but Waydenfeld recounts the experience with a teenager's irrepressible curiosity and subversive humor.

"Extraordinary." — Anne Applebaum, Pulitzer Prize-winning author of *Gulag*

Maps and Shadows: A Novel
by Krysia Jopek
- Hardcover: 978-1-60772-007-2 ($19.95)
  Trade Paperback: 978-1-60772-008-9 ($14.95)
  Ebook: 978-1-60772-013-3 ($9.99)
- 160 pages. Eleven black and white illustrations and map; Bibliography; Reading Group Guide.
- Fiction.
- **Winner of 2011 Benjamin Franklin SILVER Award for Historical Fiction.**

Stunning debut novel from poet Jopek illuminates a little known chapter of WWII—the Soviet deportations of 1.5 million Polish civilians to forced labor camps in Siberia. Told from the points of view of four members of one family, *Maps and Shadows* traces their journeys from Poland to Siberia, on divergent paths to Persia, Palestine and Italy, to Uzbekistan and Africa, converging in England and finally settling in the U.S. Fresh stylistic approach fuses minimalist narrative with lush lyricism.

"Jopek…shows how very talented she is." — *Nightreader*

The Mermaid and the Messerschmitt: War Through a Woman's Eyes, 1939-1940

by Rulka Langer

- Hardcover: 978-1-60772-000-3 ($29.95)
  Trade Paperback: 978-1-60772-001-0 ($19.95)
  Ebook: 978- 1-60772-018-8 ($12.99)
  Audiobook: Audible.com
- 468 pages. More than 100 black and white photos, maps and illustrations; contextualizing historical material; Reading Group Guide (included in paperback; online for hardcover).
- Nonfiction.
- A Selection of the **Book-of-the-Month Club,** the **History Book Club** and the **Military Book Club.**
- **Winner of 2010 Benjamin Franklin SILVER Award for Best First Book (Nonfiction).**

Thoroughly modern, Vassar-educated career woman Langer risked her life and relied on her wits to keep her two small children and elderly mother out of harm's way in Warsaw during the first six months of WWII. Engaging, clear-eyed chronicle sparkles. **"Absolutely one of the best." — Alan Furst, bestselling author of** *The Foreign Correspondent* **and** *The Spies of Warsaw*

Siege: World War II Begins

Filmed and narrated by Julien Bryan

- DVD Video, all regions: 978-1-60772-006-5 ($14.95)
- Black and white newsreel, newly restored
  (10-minute run time); plus Special Features:
  26 color screens of text, still photos and maps; historic
  4-minute audio essay by Julien Bryan for
  Edward R. Murrow's 1950s radio show "This I Believe."

A "must have" for every WWII collection! First time available on DVD. This rare historic newsreel was among the first WWII film footage to come out of Europe. Renowned American photojournalist Julien Bryan's gut-wrenching images of the Siege of Warsaw in September 1939 shocked the American public into awareness of the devastation of modern warfare and the looming danger posed by Nazi Germany. **Nominated for an Oscar** in 1940. **Inducted into the U.S. National Film Registry** in 2006 as one of the nation's most "culturally, historically or aesthetically significant films."

AQUILA POLONICA®
www.AquilaPolonica.com

Early Praise for Echoes of Tattered Tongues...

"Powerful...Deserves attention and high regard. To read these poems is to lift the lid on history and risk a step inside. One not only suffers the furnace but also endures, like the poet himself, the human will to counter history's inferno with an awful fire all its own. The poet's spare voice sings as austerely as his parents' trunk cobbled of Buchenwald wallboards. These poems do not flinch even as they take and give a punch: each note the pitch of absence given body, each silence a terrible waiting answered by singed arrival."
— **Kevin Stein, Poet Laureate of Illinois**

"Deeply moving. John Guzlowski has written a powerful, lasting, and sometimes shocking book, one in which prose and poetry join hands to document a felt comprehension of the horrors perpetrated by the Nazis in WWII. He tells the stories his parents would have told had they not been living them. Thus these pages honor his forebears and indeed all those who were in the camps. The stories will haunt you but we must read them or fail to grasp what humans can do to humans. Anyone who wishes to consider himself or herself knowledgeable about the world in which, for better or for worse, we live, will read this superb book."
— **Kelly Cherry, Poet Laureate of Virginia, 2010–2012**

"A wonderful book and a very important one. Unwaveringly lucid and luminous poems...leave his readers with no safe perches yet show them how to mourn and praise. Extraordinary."
— **Charles Adès Fishman, editor of *Blood to Remember: American Poets on the Holocaust*; poetry editor of *PRISM: An Interdisciplinary Journal for Holocaust Educators***

"A searing memoir."
— *Shelf Awareness*

"Devastating, one-of-a-kind collection."
— *Foreword Reviews*

"John Guzlowski's rugged poems rise like a land-bridge emerging from would-be oblivion to connect continents, generations, and a deeply felt personal present with the tragic, implacable history of the twentieth century."
— **Stuart Dybek, award-winning MacArthur Fellow and poet, author of *Ecstatic Cahoots: Fifty Short Stories***

"These are poems whose images and metaphors have undergone the finest grinding, becoming cyrstal lenses to magnify the inner and outer lives of his parents. The clear poetic/narrative voice is remarkably strong yet elegant—this is not a random collection but the story of a family across generations dealing with the consequences of world war. We have through Guzlowski's persona a refugee child trying to make sense of the world with parents trying to make sense of their lives after the war's work camp. Guzlowski's book is a magnificent elegy to civilian lives lost or shattered in war and thereafter. Guzlowski has successfully undertaken a monumental, moral obligation."
— *Bibliotekos*

"I could not praise it enough—masterfully done. Reads almost like a novel."
— **Gregory F. Tague, editor of *Battle Runes: Writings on War* and *Common Boundary: Stories of Immigration***

"This is a book to hold and to hug, to stroke softly... it shines...like seeing into people's souls."
— **Martin Stepek, award-winning poet, author of *For There Is Hope***

Praise for John Guzlowski's Prior Work

"Exceptional…even astonished me…reveals an enormous ability for grasping reality."
— **Nobel Laureate Czesław Miłosz on Guzlowski's poetry in *Language of Mules***

"Remarkable blend of academic scrutiny with stark, uncompromising humanity. What I find fascinating is Guzlowski's ability to always say something new…balancing overarching social commentary with the smallest, heart-wrenching details."
— **Michael Meyerhofer, *Atticus Review***

"Guzlowski should join the annals of the great recording angels, not just for his unsparing yet compassionate language but also because he makes clear what is so easy to forget: that no matter how many years pass, such events never do."
— **Lola Haskins, author of *Desire Lines: New and Selected Poems***

"Brings us face to face with what we cannot allow ourselves to forget."
— **Jared Carter, author of *Work, for the Night Is Coming* and *After the Rain***

Echoes of
Tattered Tongues

M E M O R Y   U N F O L D E D

Watch the
BOOK TRAILER

Shelf Awareness Book Trailer of the Day

www.polww2.com/EchoesTrailer